Marx's Capital

Abridged by Otto Rühle

Marx's Capital

Abridged by Otto Rühle

Printed by Imprint Digital, Exeter EX5 5HY
ISBN: 978-1-909639-39-3

Published 2017 by Workers' Liberty

20E Tower Workshops
Riley Road
London SE1 3DG
020 7394 8923
awl@workersliberty.org
www.workersliberty.org

Introduction

Otto Rühle was the second, after Karl Liebknecht, of the German Social Democratic Party's parliamentary deputies to rebel after August 1914 against the long-sacred party discipline which had at first made them vote for war credits in World War One. He was a member of the Spartacus League led by Rosa Luxemburg, and then of the early German Communist Party.

He quit the Communist Party in 1920 as part of a left opposition, some of the "left-wing communists" whom Lenin attempted to reason with and persuade in his pamphlet *Left-wing Communism, an Infantile Disorder*, and later worked with anarchistic and anarcho-syndicalist groups.

Exiled in Mexico after the Nazi seizure of power, he had friendly relations with Leon Trotsky despite the political differences which both of them disputed keenly. He served on the Dewey Commission which investigated the Moscow Trial charges against Trotsky.

And he compiled the abridged version of Marx's *Capital* which we reprint here. We have added, as appendices, four short passages from *Capital* which we consider important even for the beginning reader, but omitted by Rühle, and we have changed the chapter numbering in Rühle's text to fit with current English editions.

The abridged version was published in 1939 with a foreword by Trotsky, frequently republished under the title "Marxism in our time". Trotsky wrote: "The abridgement of the first volume of *Capital* – the foundation of Marx's entire system of economics – was made by Mr. Otto Rühle with great care and with profound understanding of his task. First to be eliminated were obsolete examples and illustrations, then quotations from writings which today are only of historic interest, polemics with writers now forgotten, and finally numerous documents – Acts of Parliament, reports of factory inspectors, and the like – which, whatever their importance for understanding a given epoch, have no place in a concise exposition that pursues theoretical rather than historical objectives.

"At the same time, Mr. Rühle did everything to preserve continuity in the development of the scientific analysis as well as unity of exposition. Logical deductions and dialectic transitions of thought have not, we trust, been infringed at any point".

Marx laboured for over 15 years on the social and economic analysis summed up in *Capital*. He produced a vast mass of drafts, the rest of which were published after his death under the titles *Grundrisse*, *Capital* volume 2, *Capital* volume 3, and *Theories of Surplus Value* volumes 1-3 (sometimes collectively labelled *Capital* volume 4). In fact, as he wrote in a letter in 1877, he did rough drafts of the later volumes before the first: "I began *Capital* privately precisely in the opposite order (beginning with the third... section) to that in which the public received it". *Capital* volume 1 is the only part of the work which he completed for publication. Some important and influential parts of Marx's work on economic theory are contained in the drafts he left uncompleted: his ideas on capitalist crises for example (mostly in *Theories of Surplus Value* volume 2), and on capitalist finance (*Capital* volumes 2 and 3).

Marx was writing to Engels with questions about capitalist accounting procedures which he needed answered for volume 2 even while volume 1 was at the printers. However, *Capital* volume 1 reads as if Marx really knew that he was unlikely to finish the whole project which he had sketched out for himself in the 1850s. Comparison between it and the volumes compiled from his drafts shows that he did enormous work on polishing and tightening up *Capital* volume 1, and included in it material which he thought vital to have published even if not strictly speaking within the scope of a first volume.

Rosa Luxemburg's comment that *Capital* volume 1 showed "not a trace of theoretical incompleteness" is exaggerated. In chapter 11, for example, Marx explicitly promises that he will elsewhere analyse how prices will systematically diverge from being proportional to values even in free-flowing markets. He had already done that analysis (though imperfectly, I think) in a never-finalised draft for volume 3. Nevertheless, Luxemburg is right that *Capital* volume 1 was written as a relatively finished and rounded whole.

As Karl Korsch remarked: "The investigation Marx undertakes in the first volume is only formally limited to the productive process of capitalism. In actual fact, in his treatment of this aspect, Marx grasps and portrays the totality of the capitalist mode of production, and the bourgeois society that emerges from it".

Capital volume 1 does not start a story, and break off midway, for the punchlines to come in the other volumes. It is not entirely self-contained, but it is more self-contained than would appear from it being labelled as volume 1 of a four-volume work.

It is not forbiddingly technical. In the preface to the first (German) edition of the book, Marx wrote: "With the exception of the section on value-form [originally included as an appendix; chapter 1 section 3 in later editions] this volume cannot stand accused on the score of difficulty. I presuppose, of course, a reader who is willing to learn something new and therefore to think for himself". In the preface to the French edition, Marx applauded the publisher's decision to put out initially as a serial. "In this form the book will be more accessible to the working class, a consideration which to me outweighs everything else".

Marx conceded that: "the method of analysis which I have employed, and which had not previously been applied to economic subjects, makes the reading of the first chapters rather arduous, and it is to be feared that the French public, always impatient to come to a conclusion, eager to know the connexion between general principles and the immediate questions that have aroused their passions, may be disheartened because they will be unable to move on at once".

He responded: "That is a disadvantage I am powerless to overcome, unless it be by forewarning and forearming those readers who zealously seek the truth. There is no royal road to science, and only those who do not dread the fatiguing climb of its steep paths have a chance of gaining its luminous summits".

To this day, *Capital* remains unique in its approach to economic analysis, and a still-fresh inspiration.

As Marx conceded, chapters 1 to 7 are fairly abstract. They develop basic concepts: use-value (utility), exchange-value (price), and value (labour-time) of commodities; concrete labour and abstract labour; money; capital; surplus-value; and labour-power (as distinct from labour).

The rest of the book analyses how capital shapes and reshapes the labour-process to extract more surplus-value, and analysing the shape that the endless spiral of accumulating more and more surplus value gives to society and its development.

Chapters 8 and 9 are transitional and fairly technical.

Chapters 10 to 15 are more empirical, and deal with how capital shapes and reshapes labour. Chapter 15 is the longest chapter in the book, and its centrepiece: it traces how developed capitalism generates a working class which gains increasing versatility and variety, but is condemned to increasingly parcellised, insecure, alienated labour, and thus it "matures the contradictions and antagonisms of the capitalist form of production and provides, along with the elements for the formation of a new society, the forces for exploding the old one".

Chapter 10 is also a long and pivotal chapter. Chapters 10 to 15 deal with: the drive to lengthen the working day, and workers' resistance (this is where the book first starts to deal with class struggle); cooperation; collective workshop production with handicraft technology (which Marx calls "manufacture"); and factory production with machines. In the course of chapter 15 the book first starts to deal with the socialistic and revolutionary impulse of class struggle.

Chapter 16 analyses labour further, developing the concepts of "the collective worker" and "productive" and "unproductive" labour. It, and chapters 17 and 18, also deal with some more technical stuff.

Chapters 19 to 22 deal with wages. Marx's *Wages, Price, and Profit*, written about the same time, gives more coverage on wages, and develops some ideas not spelled out much in *Capital*.

So far the book has been dealing with capitalist production as seen, so to speak, through the cross-section of a single week. Chapters 23 to 25 deal with the dynamics and patterns of development generated by the continuing movement of capital from week to week and year to year. It broadens out the theory, to some extent, from the workplace to the society as a whole.

Chapter 25 is the longest chapter after chapter 15, and almost as central. Chapter 32 could have been placed directly after chapter 25: it sums up from that chapter, and spells out the conclusions about the conflict-ridden nature of capitalism and the socialistic and revolutionary impulse of working-class struggle.

Right from chapter 1, Marx was at pains to stress that capitalism is a transient, historically specific mode of production. Chapters 26 to 31 are about how capitalism got going in the first place.

Chapter 33, not included in Rühle's abridgement, is an add-on, about Australia, apparently included chiefly so that lazy censors, who skim-read only the first and last chapters, would let the book past the censorship.

Marx himself once suggested that a reader new to *Capital* might start with the exciting and very down-to-earth chapter 10 — about the class struggle over the working day — rather than with chapter 1. So why did Marx nevertheless start with relatively difficult and abstract discussions?

In both his *1844 Manuscripts* and *Wage Labour and Capital*, his 1840s efforts at analysing the capitalist economy, Marx started with wages, which in *Capital* do not appear until chapter 6 (in abstract outline) or chapter 19 (in more detail). In *Capital,* as in the short book *Contribution to the Critique of Political Economy* which he published in 1859 as a sort of "first installment" of *Capital,* Marx started more abstractly and abstrusely, with "the commodity". There was a political purpose. Explaining the *Contribution* to Engels, Marx wrote that in it "the Proudhonist socialism now fashionable in France — which wants to retain private production while organising the exchange of private products, to have commodities but not money [it was a sort of socialism of workers' cooperatives, trading with each other in a market which Proudhon thought he could make fair] — is demolished to its very foundations. Communism must above all rid itself of this 'false brother'…"

Through polemics and debates, Marx had convinced himself that the root of exploitation – the root reason for the facts of wages being so wretched and the condition of the worker so oppressed with which he had started previous economic writings – lay in the very cell structure of capitalist society, in it being dominated by all-embracing commodity exchange.

He wanted to radicalise socialism, to liberate it from bourgeois prejudices, to convert it from a doctrine of improved economic fairness to one of human emancipation. He wanted to avoid starting with wages and gearing the reader into thinking "aha, wages are low, so the essential problem is, what can we do to raise them?" He wanted to point towards the conclusion of abolishing the wages system rather than reforming it.

In chapters 1 to 6 Marx reconstructs his polemical arguments in the form of positive exposition, with polemic relegated to footnotes.

Much of the argument is deliberately compressed and "flattened" in an attempt at clarity (and, understandably, reads even more "flattened" in abridgement). In reading chapters 1 to 6, especially, we have to hold our breath, as it were. Marx wants to show how just two facts – generalised commodity exchange, and the conversion of labour-power into a commodity – must generate the basic profit-accumulating, labour-subjugating mechanism of capitalism. He wants to show that those facts are not given by nature, but signify a particular and transient phase of human society.

He tries to convince us that many things which we take for granted, because they have surrounded us from early childhood, are problematic, and in fact full of conflicts and anomalies. He endeavours to persuade us that any serious attempt to combat the "abuses" of capitalism must seek to change those basic facts of market supremacy and labour-for-wages, and that those facts can be changed because they are historically transient and full of internal conflicts.

Thus, for example, in chapter 1 sections 1 and 2 he abstracts from the existence of wages and even the existence of money. In chapter 1 section 3 he will show that money is not, as myth would have it, a technical convenience invented to facilitate natural human activities, but the product of special and conflict-packed social relations.

Karl Korsch argued: "We should be deceiving ourselves if we were to think we could find a less strenuous access to *Capital* by reading it, so to speak, 'backwards' rather than from beginning to end. Not that it would be impossible to read it like that. If we did, we should certainly be spared, for example... the discovery in Chapter 16 after working through a similarly 'abstracted' treatment of the laws of relative surplus-value in the preceding chapters, that 'from one standpoint any distinction between absolute and relative surplus-value appears illusory' inasmuch as it transpires that 'relative surplus-value is absolute, and absolute surplus-value is relative'..."

But Marx's "is a method which leaves nothing out of account, but which refuses to accept things uncritically on the strength of a superficial common-or-garden empiricism soaked in prejudice... [that knows] beneath the surface of this immediate reality there lies a profounder dimension, more difficult to grasp, but just as real; a dimension that embraces not only the given reality itself, but also its continual alteration, its origins, development and demise, its transition to new forms of life in the future, and the laws governing all these changes and developments..."

Again and again we read "an initially rather abstract treatment of a given object or nexus, and the subsequent, increasingly concrete, treatment of the self-same phenomenon. This mode of development, which characterizes the whole structure of Marx's *Capital*, seems to reverse, or to 'stand on its head' the order in which given realities are 'naturally' regarded by the non-scientific observer. There is, as Marx declares repeatedly, no concept of wages in his analysis before the nineteenth chapter; there is only the concept of the value (and sometimes the price) of the 'commodity labour-power'. Not until Chapter 19 is the new concept of 'wages', which 'appears on the surface of bourgeois society as the price of labour', 'deduced' from the preparatory concept".

In *Capital*, Marx's approach is ruthless, but careful and patient, criticism of previously-developed theory. He develops his own ideas to a large degree through polemic, and at the same time insists on acknowledging it whenever he picks up an idea from a previous writer.

For the core arguments in *Capital*, mostly Marx worked through the writings of political economists, Adam Smith, David Ricardo, and others. That was because he considers their work important, and also, I guess, because at the time economic statistics were scant. Marx devoured what statistical material he could get – Thomas Tooke's *History of Prices*, the journalistic coverage of the Economist magazine, the reports of inquiries into the Bank Act, the reports of factory inspectors – and it was a vast volume, but patchy. For getting an overall picture of economic life, the only starting point was the debates of the political economists.

He also referred heavily though less obviously to the work of previous socialists, especially Pierre-Joseph Proudhon, Robert Owen, and the English and Irish Ricardian socialists such as William Thompson.

Otto Rühle's abridgement achieves its brevity mainly by omitting much of the statistical material, which is now dated, and the polemics against writers of Marx's time. That makes it an excellent starting-point for readers who want to get the gist of Marx's theory and find the length of the full book forbidding. They should however remember that the statistical citations and the polemics in the original were not padding, but integral to Marx's method.

According to a 1908 pamphlet by Karl Kautsky, Marx drew on a third main source besides the political economists like Smith and Ricardo and the socialists of the earlier 19th century. That was German critical philosophy. Kautsky's argument has been made more famous by being adapted in a 1913 pamphlet by Lenin, and repeated for example by David Harvey, the most-read contemporary commentator on *Capital*.

Indeed, Marx's academic training was in philosophy, and the influence of that training is apparent in the way he wrote *Capital*. It is more questionable whether Hegelian or post-Hegelian philosophy was a "source" in the same way as Smith, Ricardo, Proudhon, Owen, Thompson were. Hegel is quoted a good few times in *Capital*, but often, in my view always, as a joke or in a literary flourish. Nowhere is Hegel cited as a source for a substantive argument, or taken as a chopping-block for enlightening polemic.

Before Marx became a communist he moved in circles whose leftish-democratic politics were thought of as "left-Hegelian" or "young-Hegelian" because, in the repressive German states of the time, the main vent for radical thought was radical criticism of Christian religion, in which the main figures were David Strauss and Ludwig Feuerbach. Feuerbach had been a student of Hegel's, but became known in the early 1840s as the writer who had, in the words of Engels, "exploded the system" of Hegel; Strauss also studied in the philosophy department at Berlin university, where Hegel had been professor, though Hegel died just as Strauss arrived there. In Marx's early writings, the word "Hegelian" is an adjective of censure and dismissal, as when he describes Proudhon's account of history as "Hegelian trash". He completely accepted the critique of Hegel and of Hegel's dialectics by Feuerbach.

Feuerbach argued against Hegel that: "Dialectics is not a monologue that speculation carries on with itself, but a dialogue between speculation and empirical reality. A thinker is a dialectician only in so far as he is his own opponent".

Further: "The absolute philosopher [that is, Hegel] said, or at least thought of himself — naturally as a thinker and not as a man — 'La vérité c'est moi', in a way analogous to the absolute monarch claiming, 'L'État c'est moi', or the absolute God claiming, 'L'être c'est moi'. The human philosopher, on the other hand, says: Even in thought, even as a philosopher, I am a man in togetherness with men. The true dialectic is not a monologue of the solitary thinker with himself. It is a dialogue between 'I' and 'You'...".

Marx concurred. He wrote a brief but sharp *Critique of the Hegelian Dialectic* in one of his notebooks from Paris, in 1844. Marx tried to go further, in his *Theses on Feuerbach*; but to go further, not to regress to Hegel.

David Harvey, however, in some passages presents Marx's approach as a sort of modification of a sort of super-scientific scheme, allegedly derived from Hegel, which Harvey takes to be "thesis, antithesis, synthesis". In fact Hegel never used that phrase, or anything equivalent.

Marx is often described, and often described himself, as having a "materialist" approach. Broadly, that means starting from material reality rather than taking ideas to be the basic reality.

Beware of too simple an understanding of the word "materialism"! At first sight it seems easy to counterpose material reality to ideas. Here we have, say, a rock, tangible, visible, massy, measurable; there we have the idea of beauty, a mental construct. Yet in Marx's theory of capitalist production, many of the basic realities are "material" in a sense other than being physical and tangible. And Marx emphasises that.

Value (congealed labour-time) has a "phantom-like objectivity". Price is an "ideal form". Capital is not a thing, but a social relation. And so on.

A glance at modern science confirms that the definition of material reality is not straightforward. Many everyday things are not measurable. Area can never be measured, only calculated, and in fact for every physical expanse we can calculate only the area of some geometric ("ideal") approximation. Many lengths (coastlines, for example) cannot even be properly approximated, let alone measured. It is in principle impossible to measure both the position and the momentum of a sub-atomic particle simultaneously and exactly.

From the standpoint of modern mathematics, "real" numbers are as imaginary as "imaginary" numbers like the square root of minus one, and "imaginary" numbers are as real as "real" numbers.

Some everyday "real" things are quite intangible: a kilowatt hour, for example, or a bit of computer software. Some elementary particles, photons for example, have no mass. We should not take "materialism" to mean that only physical, tangible, massy, measurable things constitute reality.

Commodities are not necessarily physical and tangible. Most of the examples of commodities which Marx cites are physical (linen, iron, and so on), but he also cites labour-power as a commodity, and later on in *Capital* he choses a teacher in a fee-charging school (selling education as a commodity) as his example of a capitalistically productive worker (in contrast to a teacher in a state school, who is capitalistically unproductive).

Value (congealed labour-time) and price (exchange-value) are both realities, at different levels, and neither is quite "tangible".

Marx's "materialism" did not mean a naive belief that only the tangible is real. Nor a crude assumption that ideas rooted in society are unreal. It meant his method being different from that of the utopian socialists who saw the society around them as a product of error, and the future society as the product of the intellectual correction that they, the socialists, would bring to the populace. It was also different from that of Hegel, who saw history as the working-out of the inner logic of the eternal Idea.

Marx starts from studying social reality as it evolves, and his extrapolations for the future are derived from analysis of the conflicts built in to that reality, not from this or that ideal invoked from above. In his afterword to the second German edition of *Capital*, Marx praised a reviewer's summary of his, Marx's, method: that he tried "to show, by rigid scientific investigation, the necessity of successive determinate orders of social conditions, and to establish, as impartially as possible, the facts that serve him for fundamental starting-points". It was an inquiry that would "confine itself to the confrontation and the comparison of a facts, not with ideas, but with another fact".

When Marx writes about appearance and essence, both appearance and essence are matters of real fact – rather as a table-top is both "really" flat and solid, and "really" a swarm of whizzing electrons with vast empty spaces between them.

Marx put it very sharply in his pamphlet on the Paris Commune:

"The working class did not expect miracles from the Commune. They have no ready-made utopias to introduce by decree of the people. They know that in order to work out their own emancipation, and along with it that higher form to which present society is irresistibly tending by its own economical agencies, they will have to pass through long struggles, through a series of historic processes, transforming circumstances and people. They have no ideals to realise, but to set free the elements of the new society with which old collapsing bourgeois society itself is pregnant".

We will do best in understanding Marx's method in *Capital* if we set aside the notion that Marx was using an adaptation of a stereotype scheme, whether derived from Hegel or not, and keep in mind Marx's own words that his method was distinctive because it "regards every historically developed social form as in fluid movement, and therefore takes into account its transient nature not less than its momentary existence; because it lets nothing impose upon it, and is in its essence critical and revolutionary".

Martin Thomas

Part 1
Commodities and Money
Chapter One: Commodities

The two factors of a commodity: use value and value

The wealth of those societies in which the capitalist mode of production prevails, presents itself as "an immense accumulation of commodities," its unit being a single commodity. Our investigation must therefore begin with the analysis of a commodity.

A commodity is, in the first place, an object outside us a thing that by its properties satisfies human wants of some sort or another. The nature of such wants, whether, for instance, they spring from the stomach or from fancy, makes no difference.

Every useful thing may be looked at from the two points of view of quality and quantity. It is an assemblage of many properties and may therefore be of use in various ways. To discover the various use of things is the work of history.

The utility of a thing makes it a use-value. But this utility is not a thing of air. Being limited by the physical properties of the commodity, it has no existence apart from that commodity. A commodity, such as iron, corn, or a diamond, is therefore, so far as it is a material thing, a use-value, something useful.

Use-values become a reality only by use or consumption: they also constitute the substance of all wealth, whatever may be the social form of that wealth. They are, in addition, the material depositories of exchange value. Exchange value, at first sight, presents itself as a quantitative relation, as the proportion in which values in use of one sort are exchanged for those of another sort, a relation constantly changing with time and place.

Let us take two commodities, e.g., corn and iron. The proportions in which they are exchangeable, whatever those proportions may be, can always be represented by an equation in which a given quantity of corn is equated to some quantity of iron. What does this equation tell us? It tells us that in two different things there exists in equal quantities something common to both. The two things must therefore be equal to a third, which in itself is neither the one nor the other. Each of them, so far as it is exchange value, must therefore be reducible to this third.

This common "something" cannot be either a geometrical, a chemical, or any other natural property of commodities. Such properties claim our attention only in so far as they affect the utility of those commodities, make them use-values. But the exchange of commodities is evidently an act characterized by a total abstraction from use-value.

If then we leave out of consideration the use-value of commodities, they have only one common property left, that of being products of labour. But even the product of labour itself has undergone a change in our hands. We see in it no longer a table, a house, yarn, or any other useful thing. Its existence as a material thing is put out of sight. Neither can it any longer be regarded as the product of the labour of the joiner, the mason, the spinner, or of any other definite kind of productive labour. Along with the useful qualities of the products themselves, we put out of sight both the useful character of the various kinds of labour embodied in them, and the concrete forms of that labour; there is nothing left but what is common to them all; all are reduced to one and the same sort of labour, human labour in the abstract.

It consists of the same unsubstantial reality in each, a mere congelation of homogeneous human labour, of labour-power expended without regard to the mode of its expenditure. When looked at as crystals of this social substance, common to them all, they are — values.

A use-value, or useful article, therefore, has value only because human labour in the abstract has been embodied or materialized in it. How, then, is the magnitude of this value to be measured? Plainly, by the quantity of the value-creating substance, the labour, contained in the article.

The quantity of labour, however, is measured by its duration, and labour-time in its turn finds its standard in weeks, days, and hours. The total labour-power of society, which is embodied in the sum total of the values of all commodities produced by that society, counts here as one homogeneous mass of human labour-power, composed though it be of innumerable individual units. Each of these units is the same as any other, so far as it has the character of the average labour-power of society, and takes effect as such; that is, so far as it requires for producing a commodity, no more time than is needed on an average, no more than is socially necessary. The labour-time socially necessary is that required to produce an article under the normal conditions of production, and with the average degree of skill and intensity prevalent at the time. The introduction of power looms into England probably reduced by one half the labour required to weave a given quantity of yarn into cloth. The handloom weavers, as a matter of fact, continued to require the same time as before; but for all that, the product of one hour of their labour represented after the change only half an hour's social labour, and consequently fell to one half its former value. We see then that that which determines the magnitude of the value of any article is the amount of labour socially necessary, or the labour-time socially necessary for its production. Each individual commodity, in this connection, is to be considered as an average sample of its class.

The value of one commodity is to the value of any other, as the labour-time necessary for the production of the one is to that necessary for the production of the other. In general, the greater the productiveness of labour, the less is the labour-time required for the production of an article, the less is the amount of labour crystallized in that article, and the less is its value; and vice versa, the less the productiveness of labour, the greater is the labour-time required for the production of an article, and the greater is its value. The value of a commodity, therefore, varies directly as the quantity, and inversely as the productiveness, of the labour incorporated in it.

A thing can be a use-value, without having value. This is the case whenever its utility to man is not due to labour. Such are air, virgin soil, natural meadows, etc. A thing can be useful, and the product of human labour, without being a commodity. Whoever directly satisfies his wants with the produce of his own labour, creates, indeed, use-values, but not commodities. In order to produce the latter, he must not only produce use-values, but use-values for others, social use-values. Lastly, nothing can have value, without being an object of utility. If the thing is useless, so is the labour contained in it; the labour does not count as labour, and therefore creates no value.

The two-fold character of the labour embodied in commodities

Let us take two commodities such as a coat and 10 yards of linen, and let the former be double the value of the latter, so that, if 10 yards of linen = W, the coat = 2W.

The coat is a use-value that satisfies a particular want. Its existence is the result of a special sort of productive activity, the nature of which is determined by its aim, mode of operation, subject, means, and result. The labour, whose utility is thus represented by the value in use of its product, or which manifests itself by making its product a use-value, we call useful labour. In this connection we consider only its useful effect.

As the coat and the linen are two qualitatively different use-values, so also are the two forms of labour that produce them, tailoring and weaving. To all the different varieties of values in use there correspond as many different kinds of useful labour, classified according to the order, genus, species, and variety to which they belong in the social division of labour. This division of labour is a necessary condition for the production of commodities but it does not follow conversely, that the production of commodities is a necessary condition for the division of labour.

In a commodity, the produce of which in general takes the form of commodities, ie., in a community of commodity producers, this qualitative difference between the useful forms of labour that are carried on independently by individual producers, each on their own account, develops into a complex system, a social division of labour.

The use-values, coat, linen, &c., ie., the bodies of commodities, are combinations of two elements — matter and labour. Man can work only as Nature does, that is by changing the form of matter. Nay more, in this work of changing the form he is constantly helped by natural forces. We see, then, that labour is not the only source of material wealth, of use-values produced by labour. As William Petty puts it, labour is its father and the earth its mother.

Let us now pass from the commodity considered as a use-value to the value of commodities. By our assumption, the coat is worth twice as much as the linen. But this is a mere quantitative difference, which for the present does not concern us. We bear in mind, however, that if the value of the coat is double that of 10 yards of linen, 20 yards of linen must have the same value as one coat. So far as they are values, the coat and the linen are things of a like substance, objective expressions of essentially identical labour. But tailoring and weaving are, qualitatively, different kinds of labour. They are, however, each a productive expenditure of human brains, nerves, and muscles, and in this sense are human labour. They are but two different modes of expending human labour-power. But the value of a commodity represents human labour in the abstract, the expenditure of human labour in general.

Simple average labour, it is true, varies in character in different countries and at different times, but in a particular society it is given. Skilled labour counts only as simple labour intensified, or rather as multiplied simple labour, a given quantity of skilled being considered equal to a greater quantity of simple labour.

Just as, therefore, in viewing the coat and linen as values, we abstract from their different use-values, so it is with the labour represented by those values: we disregard the difference between its useful forms, weaving and tailoring. As the use-values, coat and linen, are combinations of special productive activities with cloth and yarn, while the values, coat and linen, are, on the other hand, mere homogeneous congelations of undifferentiated labour, so the labour embodied in these latter values does not count by virtue of its productive relation to cloth and yarn, but only as being expenditure of human labour-power.

Coats and linen, however, are not merely values, but values of definite magnitude, and according to our assumption, the coat is worth twice as much as the ten yards of linen. Whence this difference in their values? It is owing to the fact that the linen contains only half as much labour as the coat, and consequently, that in the production of the latter, labour-power must have been expended during twice the time necessary for the production of the former.

An increase in the quantity of use-values is an increase of material wealth. With two coats two men can be clothed, with one coat only one man. Nevertheless, an increased quantity of material wealth may correspond to a simultaneous fall in the magnitude of its value.

This antagonistic movement has its origin in the twofold character of labour. On the one hand all labour is, speaking physiologically, an expenditure of human labour-power, and in its character of identical abstract human labour, it creates and forms the value of commodities. On the other hand, all labour is the expenditure of human labour-power in a special form and with a definite aim, and in this, its character of concrete useful labour, it produces use-values.

I was the first to point out and to examine critically this twofold nature of the labour contained in commodities. As this point is the pivot on which a clear comprehension of political economy turns, we must go more into detail.

The form of value or exchange value

Commodities come into the world in the shape of use-values, articles, or goods. This is their plain, homely, bodily form. They are, however, commodities, only because they are something twofold, both objects of utility, and, at the same time, depositories of value. They manifest themselves therefore as commodities, or have the form of commodities, only in so far as they have two forms, a physical or natural form, and a value form. If we say that, as values, commodities are mere congelations of human labour, we reduce them by our analysis, it is true, to the abstraction, value; but we ascribe to this value no form apart from their bodily form. It is otherwise in the value relation of one commodity to another. Here, the one stands forth in its character of value by reason of its relation to the other.

The simplest value relation is evidently that of one commodity to some one other commodity of a different kind. Hence the relation between the values of two commodities supplies us with the simplest expression of the value of a single commodity.

A. Elementary or accidental form of value

1. The two poles of the expression of value — the relative form and the equivalent form

The whole mystery of the form of value lies hidden in this elementary form. Its analysis, therefore, is our real difficulty. Here two different kinds of commodities (in our example the linen and the coat), evidently play two different parts. The linen expresses its value in the coat; the coat serves as the material in which that value is expressed. The former plays an active, the latter a passive, part. The value of the linen is represented as relative value, or appears in relative form. The coat officiates as equivalent, or appears in equivalent form.

The relative form and the equivalent form are two intimately connected, mutually dependent and inseparable elements of the expression of value; but, at the same time, are mutually exclusive, antagonistic extremes — i.e., poles of the same expression. They are allotted respectively to the two different commodities brought into relation by that expression.

Whether, then, a commodity assumes the relative form, or the opposite equivalent form, depends entirely upon its accidental position in the expression of value — that is, upon whether it is the commodity whose value is being expressed or the commodity in which value is being expressed.

2. The relative form of value

a. The nature and import of this form

When occupying the position of equivalent in the equation of value, the coat ranks qualitatively as the equal of the linen, as something of the same kind, because it is value. In this position it is a thing in which we see nothing but value, or whose palpable bodily form represents value. In the production of the coat, human labour-power, in the shape of tailoring, must have been actually expended. Human labour is therefore accumulated in it. In this aspect the coat is a depository of value, but though worn to a thread, it does not let this fact show through. And as equivalent of the linen in the value equation, it exists under this aspect alone, counts therefore as embodied value, as a body that is value.

Hence, in the value equation in which the coat is the equivalent of the linen, the coat officiates as the form of value. The value of the commodity linen is expressed by the bodily form of the commodity coat, the value of one by the use-value of the other.

All that our analysis of the value of commodities has already told us, is told us by the linen itself, so soon as it comes into communication with another commodity, the coat. Only it betrays its thoughts in that language with which alone it is familiar, the language of commodities. In order to tell us that its own value is created by labour in its abstract character of human labour, it says that the coat, in so far as it is worth as much as the linen, and therefore is value, consists of the same labour as the linen. In order to inform us that its sublime reality as value is not the same as its buckram body, it says that value has the appearance of a coat, and consequently that so far as the linen is value, it and the coat are as like as two peas.

b. Quantitative determination of relative value

The equation, 20 yards of linen = 1 coat, or 20 yards of linen are worth one coat, implies that the same quantity of value-substance (congealed labour) is embodied in both; that the two commodities have each cost the same amount of labour or the same quantity of labour time. But the labour time necessary for the production of 20 yards of linen or 1 coat varies with every change in the productiveness of weaving or tailoring. We have now to consider the influence of such changes on the quantitative aspect of the relative expression of value:

I. The value of the linen may vary, that of the coat remaining constant.

II. The value of the linen may remain constant, while the value of the coat varies.

III. The quantities of labour time respectively necessary for the production of the linen and the coat may vary simultaneously in the same direction and in the same proportion.

IV. The labour time respectively necessary for the production of the linen and the coat, and therefore the value of these commodities may simultaneously vary in the same direction, but at unequal rates, or in opposite directions, or in other ways. The relative value of a commodity may vary, although its value remains constant. Its relative value may remain constant, although its value varies; finally, simultaneous variations in the magnitude of value and in that of its relative expression by no means necessarily correspond in amount.

3. The equivalent form of value

When we say that a commodity is in the equivalent form, we express the fact that it is directly exchangeable with other commodities.

The first peculiarity that strikes us, in considering the form of the equivalent, is this: use-value becomes the form of manifestation, the phenomenal form of its opposite, value. The bodily form of the commodity becomes its value form. The second peculiarity of the equivalent form is, that concrete labour becomes the form under which its opposite, abstract human labour, manifests itself.

4. The elementary form of value considered as a whole

The opposition or contrast existing internally in each commodity between use-value and value, is, therefore, made evident externally by two commodities being placed in such relation to each other, that the commodity whose value it is sought to express, figures directly as a mere use-value, while the commodity in which that value is to be expressed, figures directly as mere exchange value. Hence the elementary form of value of a commodity is the elementary form in which the contrast contained in that commodity, between use-value and value, becomes apparent.

Nevertheless, the elementary form of value passes by an easy transition into a more complete form. Therefore, according as it is placed in relation with one or the other, we get for one and the same commodity, different elementary expressions of value. The number of such possible expressions is limited only by the number of the different kinds of commodities distinct from it. The isolated expression of the value of a commodity is therefore convertible into a series, prolonged to any length, of the different elementary expressions of that value.

B. Total or expanded form of value

1. The expanded relative form of value

The linen, by virtue of the form of its value, now stands in a social relation, no longer with only one other kind of commodity, but with the whole world of commodities. As a commodity, it is a citizen of that world. At the same time, the interminable series of value equations implies, that as regards the value of a commodity, it is a matter of indifference under what particular form, or kind, of use-value it appears.

In the first form, 20 yds. of linen = 1 coat, it might for ought that otherwise appears be pure accident, that these two commodities are exchangeable in definite quantities. In the second form, on the contrary, we perceive at once the background that determines, and is essentially different from, this accidental appearance.

But in the first place, the relative expression of value is incomplete because the series representing it is interminable. In the second place, it is a many-colored mosaic of disparate and independent expressions of value. And lastly, if, as must be the case, the relative value of each commodity in turn, becomes expressed in this expanded form, we get for each of them a relative-value form, different in every case, and consisting of an interminable series of expressions of value.

2. The defects of the total or expanded form of value

The defects of the expanded relative-value form are reflected in the corresponding equivalent form. The accidental relation between two individual commodity owners disappears. It becomes plain, that it is not the exchange of commodities which regulates the magnitude of their value; but, on the contrary, that it is the magnitude of their value which controls their exchange proportions.

C. The general form of value

1. The altered character of the form of value

When a person exchanges his linen for many other commodities, and thus expresses its value in a series of other commodities, it necessarily follows, that the various owners of the latter exchange them for the linen, and consequently express the value of their various commodities in one and the same third commodity, the linen. We get a general form of value: 1 coat = 20 yards of linen, 10 lbs. of tea = 20 yards of linen, 40 lbs of coffee = 20 yards of linen, 1 quarter of corn = 20 yards of linen, 2 ounces of gold = 20 yards of linen, 1/2 a ton of iron = 20 yards of linen, x com. A, = 20 yards of linen, etc. All commodities now express their value (1) in an elementary form, because in a single commodity; (2) with unity, because in one and the same commodity.

The value of every commodity is now, by being equated to linen, not only differentiated from its own use-value, but from all other use-values generally, and is, by that very fact, expressed as that which is common to all commodities. By this form, commodities are, for the first time, effectively brought into relation with one another as values, or made to appear as exchange values.

The general value form, which represents all products of labour as mere congelations of undifferentiated human labour, shows by its very

21

structure that it is the social résumé of the world of commodities.

That form consequently makes it indisputably evident that in the world of commodities the character possessed by all labour of being human labour constitutes its specific social character.

2. The interdependent development of the relative form of value and of the equivalent form

The degree of development of the relative form of value corresponds to that of the equivalent form. But we must bear in mind that the development of the latter is only the expression and result of the development of the former. The primary relative form of value of one commodity converts some other commodity into an isolated equivalent.

The expanded form of relative value, which is the expression of the value of one commodity in terms of all other commodities, endows those other commodities with the character of particular equivalents differing in kind. And lastly, a particular kind of commodity acquires the character of universal equivalent, because all other commodities make it the material in which they uniformly express their value.

A single commodity, the linen, appears therefore to have acquired the character of direct exchangeability with every other commodity because, and in so far as, this character is denied to every other commodity. The commodity that figures as universal equivalent, is, on the other hand, excluded from the relative-value form.

3. Transition from the general form of value to the money form

The particular commodity, with whose bodily form the equivalent form is thus socially identified, now becomes the money commodity, or serves as money. It becomes the special social function of that commodity, and consequently its social monopoly, to play within the world of commodities the part of the universal equivalent.

This foremost place has been attained by one in particular — namely, gold.

D. The money form

We get the money form: 20 yards of linen = 2 ounces of gold, 1 coat = 2 ounces of gold, 10 lb. of tea = 2 ounces of gold, 40 lb. of coffee = 2 ounces of gold, 1 qr. of corn = 2 ounces of gold, 1/2 a ton of iron = 2 ounces of gold, x commodity A = 2 ounces of gold.

Gold is now money with reference to all other commodities only because it was previously, with reference to them, a simple commodity. Like all other commodities, it was also capable of serving as an equivalent, either as simple equivalent in isolated exchanges, or as particular equivalent by the side of others. Gradually it began to serve, within varying limits, as universal equivalent.

So soon as it monopolizes this position in the expression of value for the world of commodities, it becomes the money commodity, and then, and not till then, does the general form of value become changed into the money form.

The fetishism of commodities and the secret thereof

A commodity appears, at first sight, a very trivial thing, and easily understood. Its analysis shows that it is, in reality, a very queer thing, abounding in metaphysical subtleties and theological niceties. So far as it is a value in use, there is nothing mysterious about it.

It is as clear as noonday, that man, by his industry, changes the forms of the materials furnished by nature, in such a way as to make them useful to him. The form of wood, for instance, is altered, by making a table out of it. Yet, for all that the table continues to be that common, everyday thing, wood.

But, so soon as it steps forth as a commodity, it is changed into something transcendent. It not only stands with its feet on the ground, but, in relation to all other commodities, it stands on its head, and evolves out of its wooden brain grotesque ideas, far more wonderful than "table-turning" ever was.

The mystical character of commodities does not originate in their use-value. Just as little does it proceed from the nature of the determining factors of value. Whence, then, arises the enigmatical character of the product of labour, so soon as it assumes the form of commodities? Clearly from this form itself.

A commodity is therefore a mysterious thing, simply because in it the social character of men's labour appears to them as an objective character stamped upon the product of that labour; because the relation of the producers to the sum total of their own labour is presented to them as a social relation, existing not between themselves, but between the products of their labour. This is the reason why the products of labour become commodities, social things whose qualities are at the same time perceptible and imperceptible by the senses. There it is a definite social relation between men, that assumes, in their eyes, the fantastic form of a relation between things. In order, therefore, to find an analogy, we must have recourse to the mist-enveloped regions of the religious world. In that world the productions of the human brain appear as independent beings endowed with life, and entering into relation both with one another and the human race. So it is in the world of commodities with the products of men's hands. This I call the Fetishism which attaches itself to the products of labour, so soon as they are produced as commodities, and which is therefore inseparable from the production of commodities.

This fetishism of commodities has its origin in the peculiar social character of the labour that produces them. As a general rule, articles of utility become commodities, only because they are products of the labour of private individuals or groups of individuals who carry on their work independently of each other. The sum total of the labour of all these private individuals forms the aggregate labour of society. Since the producers do not come into social contact with each other until they exchange their products, the specific social character of each producer's labour does not show itself except in the act of exchange. In other words, the labour of the individual asserts itself as a part of the labour of society, only by means of the relations which the act of exchange establishes directly between the products, and indirectly, through them, between the producers. To the latter, therefore, the relations connecting the labour of one individual with that of the rest appear, not as direct social relations between individuals at work, but as what they really are, material relations between persons and social relations between things.

It is only by being exchanged that the products of labour acquire, as values, one uniform social status, distinct from their varied forms of existence as objects of utility. From this moment the labour of the individual producer acquires socially a twofold character. On the one hand, it must, as a definite useful kind of labour, satisfy a definite social want, and thus hold its place as part and parcel of the collective labour of all, as a branch of a social division of labour that has sprung up spontaneously. On the other hand, it can satisfy the manifold wants of the individual producer himself, only in so far as the mutual exchangeability of all kinds of useful private labour is an established social fact, and therefore the private useful labour of each producer ranks on an equality with that of all others.

The twofold social character of the labour of the individual appears to him, when reflected in his brain, only under those forms which are impressed upon that labour in everyday practice by the exchange of products. In this way, the character that his own labour possesses of being socially useful takes the form of the condition, that the product must be not only useful, but useful for others, and the social character that his particular labour has of being the equal of all other particular kinds of labour, takes the form that all the physically different articles that are the products of labour, have one common quality, viz., that of having value.

Hence, when we bring the products of our labour into relation with each other as values, it is not because we see in these articles the material receptacles of homogeneous human labour. Quite the contrary; whenever, by an exchange, we equate as values our different products, by that very act, we also equate, as human labour, the different kinds of labour expended upon them. We are not aware of this, nevertheless we do it. Value, therefore, does not stalk about with a label describing what it is. It is value, rather, that converts every product into a social hieroglyphic. Later on, we try to decipher the hieroglyphic, to get behind the secret of our own social products; for to stamp an object of utility as a value, is just as much a social product as language. The recent scientific discovery, that the products of labour, so far as they are values, are but material expressions of the human labour spent in their production, marks, indeed, an epoch in the history of the development of the human race, but, by no means, dissipates the mist through which the social character of labour appears to us to be an objective character of the products themselves.

When I state that coats or boots stand in a relation to linen, because it is the universal incarnation of abstract human labour, the absurdity of the statement is self-evident. Nevertheless, when the producers of coats and boots compare those articles with linen, or, what is the same thing with gold or silver, as the universal equivalent, they express the relation between their own private labour and the collective labour of society in the same absurd form. The categories of bourgeois economy consist of such like forms. They are forms of thought expressing with social validity the conditions and relations of a definite, historically determined mode of production, viz., the production of commodities. The whole mystery of commodities, all the magic and necromancy that surrounds the products of labour as long as they take the form of commodities, vanishes therefore, so soon as we come to other forms of production.

Could commodities themselves speak, they would say: Our use-value may be a thing that interests men. It is no part of us as objects. What, however, does belong to us as objects, is our value. Our natural intercourse as commodities proves it. In the eyes of each other we are nothing but exchange values. It is a peculiar circumstance that the use-value of objects is realized without exchange, by means of a direct relation between the objects and man, while, on the other hand, their value is realized only by exchange, that is, by means of a social process. Who fails here to call to mind our good friend, Dogberry, who informs neighbor Seacoal, that, "To be a well-favored man is the gift of fortune; but reading and writing comes by nature"?

Chapter Two: Exchange

It is plain that commodities cannot go to market and make exchanges of their own account. We must, therefore, have recourse to their guardians, who are also their owners. Commodities are things, and therefore without power of resistance against man. If they are wanting in docility he can use force; in other words, he can take possession of them. In order that these objects may enter into relation with each other as commodities, their guardians must place themselves in relation to one another, as persons whose will resides in those objects, and must behave in such a way that each does not appropriate the commodity of the other, and part with his own, except by means of an act done by mutual consent. They must, therefore, mutually recognise in each other the right of private proprietors. This juridical relation, which thus expresses itself in a contract, whether such contract be part of a developed legal system or not, is a relation between two wills, and is but the reflex of the real economical relation between the two. It is this economical relation that determines the subject matter comprised in each such juridical act. The persons exist for one another merely as representatives of, and, therefore, as owners of, commodities. The characters who appear on the economic stage are but the personifications of the economical relations that exist between them.

His commodity possesses for the owner no immediate use-value. Otherwise, he would not bring it to the market. It has use-value for others; for himself its only direct use-value is that of being a depository of exchange value, and consequently, a means of exchange.

Therefore, he makes up his mind to part with it for commodities whose value in use is of service to him. All commodities are non-use-values for their owners, and use-values for their non-owners.

Consequently, they must all change hands. But this change of hands is what constitutes their exchange, and the latter puts them in relation with each other as values, and realises them as values. Hence commodities must be realised as values before they can be realised as use-values. On the other hand, they must show that they are use-values before they can

26

be realised as values. For the labour spent upon them counts effectively, only in so far as it is spent in a form that is useful for others. Whether that labour is useful for others and its product consequently capable of satisfying the wants of others, can be proved only by the act of exchange.

Every owner of a commodity wishes to part with it in exchange only for those commodities whose use-value satisfies some want of his.

Looked at in this way, exchange is for him simply a private transaction. On the other hand, he desires to realise the value of his commodity, to convert it into any other suitable commodity of equal value. From this point of view, exchange is for him a social transaction of a general character. But one and the same set of transactions cannot be simultaneously for all owners of commodities both exclusively private and exclusively social and general.

The exchange of commodities, therefore, first begins on the boundaries of such communities, at their points of contact with other similar communities, or with members of the latter. So soon, however, as products once become commodities in the external relations of a community, they also, by reaction, become so in its internal intercourse. The proportions in which they are exchangeable are at first quite a matter of chance. Meantime the need for foreign objects of utility gradually establishes itself. The constant repetition of exchange makes it a normal social act. In the course of time, therefore, some portion at least of the products of labour must be produced with a special view to exchange. From that moment the distinction becomes firmly established between the utility of an object for the purposes of consumption, and its utility for the purposes of exchange. Its use-value becomes distinguished from its exchange value. On the other hand, the quantitative proportion in which the articles are exchangeable, becomes dependent on their production itself. Custom stamps them as values with definite magnitudes.

In the direct barter of products, each commodity is directly a means of exchange to its owner, and to all other persons an equivalent, but that only in so far as it has use-value for them. At this stage, therefore, the articles exchanged do not acquire a value-form independent of their own use-value. The necessity for a value-form grows with the increasing number and variety of the commodities exchanged. The problem and the means of solution arise simultaneously.

A special article, by becoming the equivalent of various other commodities, acquires at once, though within narrow limits, the character of a general social equivalent. This character comes and goes with the momentary social acts that called it into life. In turns and transiently it attaches itself first to this and then to that commodity. The particular kind of commodity to which it sticks is at first a matter of accident. Nevertheless there are two circumstances whose influence is decisive. The money-form attaches itself either to the most important articles of exchange from outside, or else it attaches itself to the object of utility that forms, like cattle, the chief portion of indigenous alienable wealth.

Man has often made man himself, under the form of slaves, serve as the primitive material of money but has never used land for that purpose. Such an idea could only spring up in a bourgeois society already well developed.

Money is a crystal formed of necessity in the course of the exchanges, whereby different products of labour are practically equated to one another and thus by practice converted into commodities. At the same rate, then, as the conversion of products into commodities is being accomplished, so also is the conversion of one special commodity into money.

An adequate form of manifestation of value, a fit embodiment of abstract, undifferentiated, and therefore equal human labour, that material alone can be whose every sample exhibits the same uniform qualities. On the other hand, since the difference between the magnitudes of value is purely quantitative, the money commodity must be susceptible of merely quantitative differences, must therefore be divisible at will, and equally capable of being re-united. Gold and silver possess these qualities by nature.

The money-form is but the reflex, thrown upon one single commodity, of the value relations between all the rest. That money is a commodity is therefore a new discovery only for those who, when they analyse it, start from its fully developed shape. The act of exchange gives to the commodity converted into money, not its value, but its specific value-form. By confounding these two distinct things some writers have been led to hold that the value of gold and silver is imaginary. The fact that money can, in certain functions, be replaced by mere symbols of itself, gave rise to that other mistaken notion, that it is itself a mere symbol.

Money, like every other commodity, cannot express the magnitude of its value except relatively in other commodities. This value is determined by the labour-time required for its production, and is expressed by the quantity of any other commodity that costs the same amount of labour-time. When it steps into circulation as money, its value is already given.

What appears to happen is, not that gold becomes money, in consequence of all other commodities expressing their values in it, but, on the contrary, that all other commodities universally express their values in gold, because it is money. The intermediate steps of the process vanish in the result and leave no trace behind.

Commodities find their own value already completely represented, without any initiative on their part, in another commodity existing in company with them. These objects, gold and silver, just as they come out of the bowels of the earth, are forthwith the direct incarnation of all human labour. Hence the magic of money. The riddle presented by money is but the riddle presented by commodities; only it now strikes us in its most glaring form.

Chapter Three: Money, or the Circulation of Commodities

The first chief function of money is to supply commodities with the material for the expression of their values, or to represent their values as magnitudes of the same denomination, qualitatively equal, and quantitatively comparable. It thus serves as a universal measure of value. And only by virtue of this function does gold, the equivalent commodity par excellence, become money.

It is not money that renders commodities commensurable. Just the contrary. It is because all commodities, as values, are realised human labour, and therefore commensurable, that their values can be measured by one and the same special commodity, and the latter be converted into the common measure of their values, i.e., into money. Money, as a measure of value, is the phenomenal form that must of necessity be assumed by that measure of value which is immanent in commodities, labour-time.

The expression of the value of a commodity in gold is its money-form or price. The price of commodities is, like their form of value generally, a form quite distinct from their palpable bodily form; it is, therefore, a purely ideal or mental form. Their owner must, therefore, lend them his tongue, or hang a ticket on them, before their prices can be communicated to the outside world. Every trader knows that it does not require the least bit of real gold to estimate in that metal millions of pounds' worth of goods.

If gold and silver are simultaneously measures of value, all commodities have two prices — one a gold-price, the other a silver-price. These exist quietly side by side, so long as the ratio of the value of silver to that of gold remains unchanged. The values of commodities are changed in imagination into so many different quantities of gold. Hence, in spite of the confusing variety of the commodities themselves, their values become magnitudes of the same denomination, gold-magnitudes. They are now capable of being compared with each other and measured, and the want becomes technically felt of comparing them with some fixed quantity of gold as a unit measure. This unit, by subsequent division into aliquot parts, becomes itself the standard or scale. Before they become money, gold, silver, and copper already possess such standard measures in their standards of weight.

As measure of value and as standard of price, money has two entirely distinct functions to perform. It is the measure of value inasmuch as it is the socially recognised incarnation of human labour; it is the standard of price inasmuch as it is a fixed weight of metal. As the measure of value it serves to convert the values of all the manifold commodities into prices, into imaginary quantities of gold; as the standard of price it measures those quantities of gold. The measure of values measures commodities considered as values; the standard of price measures, on the contrary, quantities of gold by a unit quantity of gold, not the value of one quantity of gold by the weight of another. In order to make gold a standard of price, a certain weight must be fixed upon as the unit. The less the unit is subject to variation, so much the better does the standard of price fulfil its office.

No matter how this value varies, the proportions between the values of different quantities of the metal remain constant.

A general rise in the prices of commodities can result only, either from a rise in their values — the value of money remaining constant — or from a fall in the value of money, the values of commodities remaining constant. On the other hand, a general fall in prices can result only, either from a fall in the values of commodities — the value of money remaining constant — or from a rise in the value of money, the values of commodities remaining constant. It therefore by no means follows, that a rise in the value of money necessarily implies a proportional fall in the prices of commodities; or that a fall in the value of money implies a proportional rise in prices. Such change of price holds good only in the case of commodities whose value remains constant.

By degrees there arises a discrepancy between the current money names of the various weights of the precious metal figuring as money, and the actual weights which those names originally represented. The world pound, for instance, was the money-name given to an actual pound weight of silver. When gold replaced silver as a measure of value, the same name was applied according to the ratio between the values of silver and gold, to perhaps one fifteenth of a pound of gold. The world pound, as a money-name, thus becomes differentiated from the same word as a weight-name.

Since the standard of money is on the one hand purely conventional, and must on the other hand find general acceptance, it is in the end regulated by law. A given weight of one of the precious metals, an ounce of gold, for instance, becomes officially divided into aliquot parts, with legally bestowed names, such as pound, dollar, &c. These aliquot parts, which henceforth serve as units of money, are then subdivided into other aliquot parts with legal names, such as shilling, penny, &c. But, both before and after these divisions are made, a definite weight of metal is the standard of metallic money. The sole alteration consists in the subdivision and denomination. In this way commodities express by their prices how much they are worth, and money serves as money of account whenever it is a question of fixing the value of an article in its money-form.

Price is the money-name of the labour realised in a commodity. Hence the expression of the equivalence of a commodity with the sum of money constituting its price, is a tautology, just as in general the expression of the relative value of a commodity is a statement of the equivalence of two commodities.

But although price, being the exponent of the magnitude of a commodity's value, is the exponent of its exchange-ratio with money, it does not follow that the exponent of this exchange-ratio is necessarily the exponent of the magnitude of the commodity's value. Magnitude of value expresses a relation of social production, it expresses the connection that necessarily exists between a certain article and the portion of the total labour-time of society required to produce it. As soon as magnitude of value is converted into price, the above necessary relation takes the shape of a more or less accidental exchange-ratio between a single commodity and another, the money-commodity. But this exchange-ratio may express either the real magnitude of that commodity's value, or the quantity of gold deviating from that value, for which, according to circumstances, it may be parted with.

31

The possibility, therefore, of quantitative incongruity between price and magnitude of value is inherent in the price-form itself. This is no defect, but on the contrary, admirably adapts the price-form to a mode of production whose inherent laws impose themselves only as the mean of apparently lawless irregularities that compensate one another.

The price-form may conceal a qualitative inconsistency, so much so, that, although money is nothing but the value-form of commodities, price ceases altogether to express value. Objects that in themselves are no commodities, such as conscience, honour, &c., are capable of being offered for sale by their holders, and of thus acquiring, through their price, the form of commodities. Hence an object may have a price without having value. The price in that case is imaginary, like certain quantities in mathematics. On the other hand, the imaginary price-form may sometimes conceal either a direct or indirect real value-relation; for instance, the price of uncultivated land, which is without value, because no human labour has been incorporated in it.

A price therefore implies both that a commodity is exchangeable for money, and also that it must be so exchanged. On the other hand, gold serves as an ideal measure of value, only because it has already, in the process of exchange, established itself as the money-commodity. Under the ideal measure of values there lurks the hard cash.

In so far as exchange is a process, by which commodities are transferred from hands in which they are non-use-values, to hands in which they become use-values, it is a social circulation of matter. The product of one form of useful labour replaces that of another. When once a commodity has found a resting-place, where it can serve as a use-value, it falls out of the sphere of exchange into that of consumption. But the former sphere alone interests us at present. We have, therefore, now to consider exchange from a formal point of view; to investigate the change of form or metamorphosis of commodities which effectuates the social circulation of matter.

The comprehension of this change of form is, as a rule, very imperfect. The cause of this imperfection is, apart from indistinct notions of value itself, that every change of form in a commodity results from the exchange of two commodities, an ordinary one and the money-commodity. If we keep in view the material fact alone we overlook the very thing that we ought to observe — namely, what has happened to the form of the commodity. We overlook the facts that gold, when a mere commodity, is not money, and that when other commodities express their prices in gold, this gold is but the money-form of those commodities themselves.

Commodities, first of all, enter into the process of exchange just as they are. The process then differentiates them into commodities and money, and thus produces an external opposition corresponding to the internal opposition inherent in them, as being at once use-values and values. Commodities as use-values now stand opposed to money as exchange value. On the other hand, both opposing sides are commodities, unities of use-value and value. But this unity of differences manifests itself at two opposite poles, and at each pole in an opposite way. Being poles they are as necessarily opposite as they are connected. One the one side of the equation we have an ordinary commodity, which is in reality a use-value. Its value is expressed only ideally in its price, by which it is equated to its opponent, the gold, as to the real embodiment of its value. On the other hand, the gold in its metallic reality ranks as the embodiment of value, as money. Gold, as gold, is exchange value itself. These antagonistic forms of commodities are the real forms in which the process of their exchange moves and takes place.

The exchange becomes an accomplished fact by two metamorphoses of opposite yet supplementary characters, and by the following changes in their form:

Commodity (C) — Money (M) — Commodity (C)

But the apparently single process is in reality a double one. From the pole of the commodity owner it is a sale, from the opposite pole of the money owner, it is a purchase. In other words, a sale is a purchase, C — M is also M — C. As the person who makes a sale, the owner is a seller; as the person who makes a purchase, he is a buyer.

The complete metamorphosis of a commodity, in its simplest form, implies four extremes, and three dramatis personae. First, a commodity comes face to face with money; the latter is the form taken by the value of the former, and exists in all its hard reality, in the pocket of the buyer. A commodity-owner is thus brought into contact with a possessor of money. So soon, now as the commodity has been changed into money, the money becomes its transient equivalent-form, the use-value of which equivalent-form is to be found in the bodies of other commodities. Money, the final term for the first transmutation, is at the same time the starting point for the second. The person who is a seller in the first transaction thus becomes a buyer in the second, in which a third commodity-owner appears on the scene as a seller.

The two phases, each inverse to the other, that make up the metamorphosis of a commodity constitute together a circular movement, a circuit: commodity-form, stripping off of this form, and return to the commodity-form. No doubt, the commodity appears here under two different aspects. At the starting point it is not a use-value to its owner; at the finishing point it is. So, too, the money appears in the first phase as a solid crystal of value, a crystal into which the commodity eagerly solidifies, and in the second, dissolves into the mere transient equivalent-form destined to be replaced by a use-value. The circuit made by one commodity in the course of its metamorphoses is inextricably mixed up with the circuits of other commodities. The total of all the different circuits constitutes the circulation of commodities.

Nothing can be more childish than the dogma, that because every sale is a purchase, and every purchase a sale, therefore the circulation of commodities necessarily implies an equilibrium of sales and purchases. Sale and purchase constitute one identical act, an exchange between a commodity-owner and an owner of money, between two persons as opposed to each other as the two poles of a magnet. The identity implies that the commodity is useless, if, on being thrown into the alchemistical retort of circulation, it does not come out again in the shape of money; implies that the exchange, if it does take place, constitutes a period of rest, an interval, long or short, in the life of the commodity. No one can sell unless some one else purchases. But no one is forthwith bound to purchase, because he has just sold. Circulation bursts through all restrictions as to time, place, and individuals, imposed by direct barter, and this it effects by splitting up, into the antithesis of a sale and a purchase, the direct identity. To say that these two independent and antithetical acts have an intrinsic unity, are essentially one, is the same as to say that this intrinsic oneness expresses itself in an external antithesis. If the interval in time between the two complementary phases of the complete metamorphosis of a commodity becomes too great, if the split between the sale and the purchase becomes too pronounced, their oneness asserts itself by producing — a crisis. The movement of the commodity is a circuit. On the other hand, the form of this movement precludes a circuit from being made by the money. The result is not the return of the money, but its continual removal further and further away from its starting point.

In the first phase of its circulation the commodity changes place with the money. Thereupon the commodity, under its aspect of a useful object, falls out of circulation into consumption. In its stead we have its value-shape — the money. It then goes through the second phase of its circulation, not under its own natural shape, but under the shape of money.

The continuity of the movement is therefore kept up by the money alone, and the same movement that as regards the commodity consists of two processes of an antithetical character, is, when considered as the movement of the money, always one and the same process, a continued change of places with ever fresh commodities. Hence the result brought about by the circulation of commodities, namely, the replacing of one commodity by another, takes the appearance of having been effected not by means of the change of form of the commodities, but rather by the money acting as a medium of circulation, by an action that circulates commodities, to all appearance motionless in themselves. Money is continually withdrawing commodities from circulation and stepping into their places, and in this way continually moving further and further from its starting-point.

Hence, although the movement of the money is merely the expression of the circulation of commodities, yet the contrary appears to be the actual fact, and the circulation of commodities seems to be the result of the movement of the money. Again, money functions as a means of circulation, only because in it the values of commodities have independent reality. Hence its movement, as the medium of circulation, is, in fact, merely the movement of commodities while changing their forms.

Money keeps continually within the sphere of circulation, and moves about in it. The question arises, how much money does this sphere absorb?

Since money and commodities always come bodily face to face, it is clear that the amount of the means of circulation required is determined beforehand by the sum of the prices of all these commodities. As a matter of fact, the money in reality represents the quantity or sum of gold ideally expressed beforehand by the sum of the prices of the commodities. The equality of these two sums is therefore self-evident.

We know, however, that, the values of commodities remaining constant, their prices vary with the value of gold, rising in proportion as it falls, and falling in proportion as it rises. Now if, in consequence of such a rise or fall in the value of gold, the sum of the prices of commodities fall or rise, the quantity of money in currency must fall or rise to the same extent. The change in the quantity of the circulating medium is, in this case, it is true, caused by money itself, yet not in virtue of its function as a medium of circulation, but of its function as a measure of value. First, the price of the commodities varies inversely as the value of the money, and then the quantity of the medium of circulation varies directly as the price of the commodities. Exactly the same thing would happen if, for instance, instead of the value of gold falling, gold were replaced by silver as the measure of value, or if, instead of the value of silver rising, gold were to thrust silver out from being the measure of value. In each case the value of the material of money, i.e., the value of the commodity that serves as the measure of value, would have undergone a change, and therefore, so, too would the prices of commodities which express their values in money, and so, too, would the quantity of money current whose function it is to realise those prices.

If we consider the value of gold to be given, and if now we further suppose the price of each commodity to be given, the sum of the prices clearly depends on the mass of commodities in circulation. If the mass of commodities remain constant, the quantity of circulating money varies with the fluctuations in the prices of those commodities. It increases and diminishes because the sum of the prices increases or diminishes in consequence of the change of price.

The velocity of that currency reflects the rapidity with which commodities change their forms, the continued interlacing of one series of metamorphoses with another, the hurried social interchange of matter, the rapid disappearance of commodities from the sphere of circulation, and the equally rapid substitution of fresh ones in their places. On the other hand, the retardation of the currency reflects the separation of these two processes into isolated antithetical phases, reflects the stagnation in the change of form, and therefore, in the social interchange of matter.

The total quantity of money functioning during a given period as the circulating medium, is determined, on the one hand, by the sum of the prices of the circulating commodities, and on the other hand, by the rapidity with which the antithetical phases of the metamorphoses follow one another.

The three factors, however, state of prices, quantity of circulating commodities, and velocity of money-currency, are all variable. Hence, the sum of the prices to be realised, and consequently the quantity of the circulating medium depending on that sum, will vary with the numerous variations of these three factors in combination.

That money takes the shape of coin, springs from its function as the circulating medium. The weight of gold represented in imagination by the prices or money-names of commodities, must confront those commodities, within the circulation, in the shape of coins or pieces of gold of a given denomination. Coining, like the establishment of a standard of prices, is the business of the State.

During their currency, coins wear away, some more, others less. Name and substance, nominal weight and real weight, begin their process of separation. Coins of the same denomination become different in value, because they are different in weight.

This fact implies the latent possibility of replacing metallic coins by tokens of some other material, by symbols serving the same purposes as coins.

The tokens keep company with gold, to pay fractional parts of the smallest gold coin. The weight of metal in the silver and copper tokens is arbitrarily fixed by law. When in currency, they wear away even more rapidly than gold coins. Therefore things that are relatively without value, such as paper notes, can serve as coins in its place. We allude here only to inconvertible paper money issued by the State and having compulsory circulation.

Some one may ask why gold is capable of being replaced by tokens that have no value. But it is capable of being so replaced only in so far as it functions exclusively as coin, or as the circulating medium, and as nothing else. Each piece of money is a mere coin, or means of circulation, only so long as it actually circulates. The minimum mass of gold remains constantly within the sphere of circulation, continually functions as a circulating medium, and exists exclusively for that purpose. Its movement therefore represents nothing but the continued alternation of the inverse phases of the metamorphosis C — M — C, phases in which commodities confront their value-forms, only to disappear again immediately. The independent existence of the exchange value of a commodity is here a transient apparition, by means of which the commodity is immediately replaced by another commodity. Hence, in this process which continually makes money pass from hand to hand, the mere symbolical existence of money suffices. Its functional existence absorbs, so to say, its material existence. Being a transient and objective reflex of the prices of commodities, it serves only as a symbol of itself, and is therefore capable of being replaced by a token. One thing is, however, requisite; this token must have an objective social validity of its own, and this the paper symbol acquires by its forced currency.

But as soon as the series of metamorphoses is interrupted, as soon as sales are not supplemented by subsequent purchases, money becomes petrified into a hoard. Hoarding serves various purposes in the economy of the metallic circulation. In order that the mass of money, actually current, may constantly saturate the absorbing power of the circulation, it is necessary that the quantity of gold and silver in a country be greater than the quantity required to function as coin. This condition is fulfilled by money taking the form of hoards. These reserves serve as conduits for the supply or withdrawal of money to or from the circulation, which in this way never overflows its banks. The development of money into a medium of payment makes it necessary to accumulate money against the dates fixed for the payment of the sums owing. While hoarding, as a distinct mode of acquiring riches, vanishes with the progress of civil society, the formation of reserves of the means of payment grows with that progress.

Credit-money springs directly out of the function of money as a means of payment. Certificates of the debts owing for the purchased commodities circulate for the purpose of transferring those debts to others.

When the production of commodities has sufficiently extended itself, money begins to serve as the means of payment beyond the sphere of the circulation of commodities. It becomes the commodity that is the universal subject-matter of all contracts. When money leaves the home sphere of circulation, it strips off the local garbs which it there assumes, of a standard of prices, of coin, of tokens, and of a symbol of value, and returns to its original form of bullion. In the trade between the markets of the world, the value of commodities is expressed so as to be universally recognised. Hence their independent value-form also, in these cases, confronts them under the shape of universal money. It is only in the markets of the world that money acquires to the full extent the character of the commodity whose bodily form is also the immediate social incarnation of human labour in the abstract.

Part 2
The Transformation of Money into Capital
Chapters Four, Five, and Six: The General Formula for Capital. The Buying and Selling of Labour-Power

The circulation of commodities is the starting point of capital. The production of commodities, their circulation, and that more developed form of their circulation called commerce, these form the historical groundwork from which it rises. The modern history of capital dates from the creation in the 16th century of a world-embracing commerce and a world-embracing market.

All new capital, to commence with, comes on the stage that is, on the market, whether of commodities, labour, or money, even in our days, in the shape of money that by a definite process has to be transformed into capital.

The first distinction we notice between money that is money only, and money that is capital, is nothing more than a difference in their form of circulation. The simplest form of the circulation of commodities is C-M-C, the transformation of commodities into money, and the change of the money back again into commodities; or selling in order to buy. But alongside of this form we find another specifically different form: M-C-M, the transformation of money into commodities, and the change of commodities back again into money; buying in order to sell. Money that circulates in the latter manner is thereby transformed into, becomes capital and is already potentially capital.

In the first phase, M-C, or the purchase, the money changed into a commodity. In the second phase, C-M or the sale, the commodity is changed back again into money. The result, in which the phases of the process vanish, is the exchange of money for money, M-M.

The circuit M-C-M would be absurd and without meaning if the intention were to exchange by this means two equal sums of money.

In the circulation C-M-C, the money is in the end converted into a commodity, that serves as a use-value; it is spent once for all. The circuit M-C-M, on the contrary, commences with money and ends with money.

Its leading motive, and the goal that attracts it, is therefore mere exchange value. One sum of money is distinguishable from another only by its amount. The character and tendency of the process M-C-M, is therefore not due to any qualitative difference: between its extremes, but solely to their quantitative difference. The exact form of this process is therefore M-C- M', where M' = M + ΔM = the original sum advanced, plus an increment. This increment or excess over the original value I call "surplus-value". The value originally advanced, therefore, not only remains intact while in circulation, but adds to itself a surplus-value or expands itself. It is this movement that converts it into capital.

The simple circulation of commodities — selling in order to buy — is a means of carrying out a purpose unconnected with circulation, namely, the satisfaction of wants. The circulation of money as capital is, on the contrary, an end in itself, for the expansion of value takes place only within this constantly renewed movement. The circulation of capital has therefore no limits. Thus the conscious representative of this movement the possessor of money becomes a capitalist. His person, or rather his pocket, is the point from which the money starts and to which it returns. The expansion of value, which is the objective basis or main-spring of the circulation, becomes his subjective aim. It functions as capital personified and endowed with consciousness and a will. The restless never-ending process of profit-making alone is what he aims at.

This boundless greed after riches, this passionate chase after exchange-value, is common to the capitalist and the miser; but while the miser is merely a capitalist gone mad, the capitalist is a rational miser. The never ending augmentation of exchange-value, which the miser strives after, by seeking to save his money from circulation, is attained by the more acute capitalist, by constantly throwing it afresh into circulation.

Value therefore now becomes value in process, money in process, and, as such, capital. It comes out of circulation, enters into it again, preserves and multiplies itself within its circuit, comes back out of it with expanded bulk, and begins the same round ever afresh. M-M', money which begets money, such is the description of Capital from the mouths of its first interpreters, the Mercantilists.

The change of value that occurs in the case of money intended to be converted into capital, cannot take place in the money itself, since in its function of means of purchase and of payment, it does no more than realise the price of the commodity it buys or pays for; and, as hard cash, it is value petrified, never varying. Just as little can it originate in the resale of the commodity, which does no more than transform the article from its bodily form back again into its money-form. The change originates in the use-value of the commodity.

In order to be able to extract value from the consumption of a commodity, our friend, Moneybags, must be so lucky as to find, in the market, a commodity, whose use-value possesses the peculiar property of being a source of value, whose actual consumption, therefore, is itself an embodiment of labour, and, consequently, a creation of value.

The possessor of money does find on the market such a special commodity in capacity for labour or labour power. By it is to be understood the aggregate of those mental and physical capabilities existing in a human being, which he exercises whenever he produces a use-value of any description.

He and the owner of money meet in the market, and deal with each other as on the basis of equal rights, with this difference alone, that one is buyer, the other seller; both, therefore, equal in the eyes of the law. The continuance of this relation demands that the owner of the labour-power should sell it only for a definite period, for if he were to sell it rump and stump, once for all, he would be selling himself, converting himself from a free man into a slave, from an owner of a commodity into a commodity. He must constantly look upon his labour-power as his own property, his own commodity, and this he can only do by placing it at the disposal of the buyer temporarily, for a definite period of time. By this means alone can he avoid renouncing his rights of ownership over it.

This peculiar commodity, labour-power, like all others, has a value. How is that value determined? The value of labour-power is determined, as in the case of every other commodity, by the labour-time necessary for the production, and consequently also the reproduction, of this special article. Labour-power exists only as a capacity, or power of the living individual. Its production consequently presupposes his existence. Given the individual, the production of labour-power consists in his reproduction of himself or his maintenance. For his maintenance he requires a given quantity of the means of subsistence. Therefore the labour-time requisite for the production of labour-power reduces itself to that necessary for the production of those means of subsistence; in other words, the value of labour-power is the value of the means of subsistence necessary for the maintenance of the labourer. His means of subsistence must therefore be sufficient to maintain him in his normal state as a labouring individual.

His natural wants, such as food, clothing, fuel, and housing, vary according to the climatic and other physical conditions of his country. On the other hand, the number and extent of his so-called necessary wants, as also the modes of satisfying them, are themselves the product of historical development, and depend therefore to a great extent on the degree of civilisation of a country.

Nevertheless, in a given country, at a given period, the average quantity of the means of subsistence necessary for the labourer is practically known.

One consequence of the peculiar nature of labour power as a commodity is, that its use-value does not, on the conclusion of this contract between the buyer and seller, immediately pass into the hands of the former. Its use-value consists in the subsequent exercise of its force, in the consumption of the labour-power. In every country in which the capitalist mode of production reigns, it is the custom not to pay for labour-power before it has been exercised for the period fixed by the contract. In all cases, therefore, the use-value of the labour- power is advanced to the capitalist; he everywhere gives credit to the capitalist.

The consumption of labour-power is at one and the same time the production of commodities and of surplus value. The consumption of labour-power is completed, as in the case of every other commodity, outside the limits of the market or of the sphere of circulation, within the hidden abode of production.

Part 3
The Production of Absolute Surplus-Value
Chapter Seven: The Labour-Process and the Process Of Producing Surplus-Value

The capitalist buys labour-power in order to use it; and labour-power in use is labour itself. The purchaser of labour-power consumes it by setting the seller of it to work.

Labour is, in the first place, a process in which both man and Nature participate, and in which man of his own accord starts, regulates, and controls the material re-actions between himself and Nature. We presuppose labour in a form that stamps it as exclusively human. A spider conducts operations that resemble those of a weaver, and a bee puts to shame many an architect in the construction of her cells. But what distinguishes the worst architect from the best of bees is this, that the architect raises his structure in imagination before he erects it in reality. At the end of every labour-process, we get a result that already existed in the imagination of the labourer at its commencement. He not only effects a change of form in the material on which he works, but he also realises a purpose of his own that gives the law to his modus operandi, and to which he must subordinate his will.

The elementary factors of the labour-process are 1, the personal activity of man, i.e., work itself, 2, the subject of that work, and 3, its instruments.

All raw material is the subject of labour, but not every subject of labour is raw material; it can only become so, after it has undergone some alteration by means of labour. With the exception of the extractive industries, in which the material for labour is provided immediately by Nature, such as mining, hunting, fishing, and so on, all branches of industry manipulate raw material, objects already filtered through labour, already products of labour.

An instrument of labour is a thing, or a complex of things, which the labourer interposes between himself and the subject of his labour, and which serves as the conductor of his activity. He makes use of the mechanical, physical, and chemical properties of some substances in order to make other substances subservient to his aims. No sooner does labour undergo the least development, than it requires specially prepared instruments. In the labour-process, therefore, man's activity, with help of the instruments of labour, effects an alteration, designed from the commencement, in the material worked upon. The process disappears in the product; the latter is a use-value. Labour has incorporated itself with its subject: the former is materialised, the latter transformed. The blacksmith forges and the product is a forging. If we examine the whole process from the point of view of its result, the product, it is plain that both the instruments and the subject of labour, are means of production, and that the labour itself is productive labour.

Whether a use-value is to be regarded as raw material, as instrument of labour, or as product, this is determined entirely by its function in the labour process, by the position it there occupies.

The capitalist purchases, in the open market, all the necessary factors of the labour-process; its objective factors, the means of production, as well as its subjective factor, labour-power. He then proceeds to consume the commodity, the labour-power that he has just bought, by causing the labourer, the impersonation of that labour-power, to consume the means of production by his labour.

The labour-process, the process by which the capitalist consumes labour-power, exhibits two characteristic phenomena: first, the labourer works under the control of the capitalist to whom his labour belongs; secondly, the product is the property of the capitalist and not that of the labourer, its immediate producer. By the purchase of labour-power, the capitalist incorporates labour, as a living ferment, with the lifeless constituents of the product. From his point of view, the labour process is nothing more than the consumption of the commodity purchased, i.e., of labour-power; but this consumption cannot be effected except by supplying the labour-power with the means of production.

The aim of the capitalist is to produce not only a use-value, but a commodity also; not only use-value, but value; not only value, but at the same time surplus value.

Just as commodities are, at the same time, use-values and values, so the process of producing them must be a labour-process, and at the same time, a process of creating value.

If the process of producing value be not carried beyond the point where the value paid by the capitalist for the labour-power is replaced by an exact equivalent, it is simply a process of producing value; if it be continued beyond that point, it becomes a process of creating surplus-value.

The value of a day's labour-power amounts to 3 shillings, because the means of subsistence that are daily required of the production of labour-power, cost half a day's labour. The value of labour-power and the value which that labour power creates in the labour process, are two entirely different magnitudes; and this difference of the two values what the capitalist had in view, when he was purchasing the labour power. The useful qualities that labour-power possesses, and by virtue of which it makes yarn or boots, where to him nothing more than a conditio sine qua non; for in order to create value, labour must be expended in a useful manner. What really influenced him was the specific use-value which this commodity possesses of being a source not only of value, but of more value than it has itself. This is the special service that the capitalist expects from labour-power, and in this transaction he acts in accordance with the "eternal laws" of the exchange of commodities. The seller of labour-power, like the seller of any other commodity, realises its exchange value, and parts with its use-value. He cannot take the one without given the other.

The use-value of labour-power, or in other words, labour, belongs just as little to its seller, as the use-value of oil after it has been sold belongs to the dealer who has sold it. The owner of the money has paid the value of a day's labour power; his, therefore, is the use of it for a day; a day's labour belongs to him. The circumstance, that on the one hand the daily sustenance of labour power costs only half a day's labour, while on the other hand the very same labour-power can work during a whole day, that consequently the value which its use during one day creates, is double what he pays for that use, this circumstance is, without doubt, a piece of good luck for the buyer, but by no means an injury to the seller.

The labourer therefore finds, in the workshop, the means of production necessary for working, not only during six, but during twelve hours. The capitalist, as buyer, paid for each commodity, for the cotton, the spindle and the labour-power, its full value. Equivalent was exchanged for equivalent. He then did what is done by every purchaser of commodities; he consumed their use-value. The consumption of the labour-power, which was also the process of producing commodities. He withdraws 3 shillings more from the circulation than he originally threw into it. This metamorphosis, this conversion of money into capital, takes place both within the sphere of circulation and also outside it; within the circulation, because conditioned by the purchase of the labour-power in the market; outside the circulation, because what is done within it is only a stepping-stone to the production of surplus-value, a process which is entirely confined to the sphere of production. By turning his money into commodities that serve as the material elements of a new product, and as factors in the labour-process, by incorporating living labour with their dead substance, the capitalists at the same time converts value, i.e., past, materialised, and dead labour into capital, into value big with value.

Viewed as a value-creating process, the same labour-process presents itself under its quantitative aspect alone. Here it is a question merely of the time occupied by the labourer in doing the work; of the period during with the labour power is usefully expended. That labour, whether previously embodied in the means of production, or incorporated in them for the first time during the process by the action of labour-power, counts in either case only according to its duration.

Moreover, only so much of the time spent in the production of any article is counted, as, under the given social conditions, is necessary. The consequences of this are various. In the first place, it becomes necessary that the labour should be carried on under normal conditions. If a self-acting mule is the implement in general use for spinning, it would be absurd to supply the spinner with a distaff and spinning wheel. The cotton too must not be such rubbish as to cause extra waste in being worked, but must be of suitable equality. Whether the material factors of the process are of normal quality or not, depends entirely upon the capitalist. Then again, the labour-power itself must be of average efficacy. In the trade in which it is being employed, it must possess the average skill, handiness and quickness prevalent in that trade, and must be applied with the average amount of exertion and with the usual degree of intensity; the capitalist is careful to see that this is done. He has bought the use of the labour-power for a definite period, and he insists upon his rights. He has no intention of being robbed. Lastly, all wasteful consumption of raw material or instruments of labour is strictly forbidden.

The process of production, considered the one hand as the unity of the labour-process and the process of creating value, is production of commodities; considered on the other hand as the unity of the labour process and the process of producing surplus-value, it is the capitalist process of production, or capitalist production of commodities.

In the creation of surplus-value it does not in the least matter, whether the labour appropriated by the capitalist be simple unskilled labour or average quality or more complicated skilled labour. All labour of a higher or more complicated character than average labour is expenditure of labour-power of a more costly kind, labour-power whose production has cost more time and labour, and which therefore has a higher value, than unskilled or simple labour-power. Its consumption is labour of a higher class, labour that creates in equal times proportionally higher values than unskilled labour does. The surplus-value results only from a quantitative excess of labour, from a lengthening-out of one and the same labour-process.

Chapter Eight: Constant Capital and Variable Capital

The various factors of the labour-process play different parts in forming the value of the product. The labourer adds fresh value to the subject of his labour by expending upon it a given amount of additional labour. On the other hand, the values of the means of production used up in the process are preserved, and present themselves afresh as constituent parts of the value of the product. The value of the means of production is therefore preserved, by being transferred to the product. This transfer takes place during the conversion of those means into a product, or in other words, during the labour-process. It is brought about by labour; but how?

Since the addition of new value to the subject of his labour, and the preservation of its former value, are two entirely distinct results, produced simultaneously by the labourer, during one operation, it is plain that this twofold nature of the result can be explained only by the twofold nature of his labour; at one and the same time, it must in one character create value, and in another character preserve or transfer value.

It is by virtue of its general character, as being expenditure of human labour-power in the abstract, that spinning adds new value to the values of the cotton and the spindle; and on the other hand, it is by virtue of its special character, as being a concrete, useful process, that the same labour of spinning both transfers the values of the means of production to the product, and preserves them in the product. Hence at one and the same time there is produced a twofold result.

So long as the conditions of production remain the same, the more value the labourer adds by fresh labour, the more value he transfers and preserves; but he does so merely because this addition of new value takes place under conditions that have not varied and are independent of his own labour. Of course, it may be said in one sense that the labourer preserves old value always in proportion to the quantity of new value that he adds.

In the labour-process the means of production transfer their value to the product only so far as along with their use-value they lose also their exchange-value. They give up to the product that value alone which they themselves lose as means of production. The maximum loss of value that they can suffer in the process is plainly limited by the amount of the original value with which they came into the process. Therefore the means of production can never add more value to the product than they themselves possess independently of the process in which they assist.

The same instrument of production takes part as a whole in the labour-process, while at the same time as an element in the formation of value, it enters only by fractions. On the other hand, a means of production may take part as a whole in the formation of value, while into the labour-process it enters only bit by bit. In the value of the product, there is a re-appearance of the value of the means of production, but there is, strictly speaking, no reproduction of that value. That which is produced is a new use-value in which the old exchange-value re-appears.

The surplus of the total value of the product, over the sum of the values of its constituent factors, is the surplus of the expanded capital over the capital originally advanced. The means of production on the one hand, labour-power on the other, are merely the different modes of existence which the value of the original capital assumed when from being money it was transformed into the various factors of the labour-process.

That part of capital which is represented by the means of production, by the raw material, auxiliary material and the instruments of labour, does not, in the process of production, undergo any quantitative alteration of value. I therefore call it the constant part of capital, or, more shortly, constant capital.

On the other hand, that part of capital, represented by labour-power, does, in the process of production, undergo an alteration of value. It both reproduces the equivalent of its own value, and also produces an excess, a surplus-value, which may itself vary, may be more or less according to circumstances. This part of capital is continually being transformed from a constant into a variable magnitude. I therefore call it the variable part of capital, or, shortly, variable capital.

The same elements of capital which, from the point of view of the labour-process, present themselves respectively as the objective and subjective factors present themselves, from the point of view of the process of creating surplus-value, as constant and variable capital.

Chapter Nine: The Rate of Surplus Value

The surplus-value generated in the process of production by C, the capital advanced, or in other words, the self-expansion of the value of the capital C, presents itself for our consideration, in the first place, as a surplus, as the amount by which the value of the product exceeds the value of its constituent element. We have seen that the labourer, during one portion of the labour-process, produces only the value of his labour power, that is, the value of his means of subsistence. Now since his work forms part of a system, based on the social division of labour, he does not directly produce the actual necessaries which he himself consumes; he produces instead a particular commodity, yarn for example, whose value is equal to the value of those necessaries or of the money with which they can be bought. The portion of his day's labour devoted to this purpose, will be greater or less, in proportion to the value of the necessaries that he daily requires on an average, or, what amounts to the same thing, in proportion to the labour-time required on an average to produce them. The portion of the working day, then, during which this reproduction takes place, I call "necessary" labour-time, and the labour expended during that time I call "necessary" labour. Necessary, as regards the labourer, because independent of the particular social form of his labour; necessary, as regards capital, and the world of capitalists, because on the continued existence of the labourer depends their existence also.

During the second period of the labour-process, that in which his labour is no longer necessary labour, the workman, it is true, labours, expends labour-power; but his labour, being no longer necessary labour, he creates no value for himself. He creates surplus-value which, for the capitalist, has all the charms of a creation out of nothing. This portion of the working day, I name surplus-labour-time, and to the labour expended during that time, I give the name of surplus-labour. It is every bit as important, for a correct understanding of surplus-value, to conceive it as a mere congelation of surplus-labour-time, as nothing but materialised surplus labour, as it is, for a proper comprehension of value, to conceive it as a mere congelation of so many hours of labour, as nothing but materialised labour.

The essential difference between the various economic forms of society, between, for instance, a society based on slave labour, and one based on wage labour, lies only in the mode in which this surplus-labour is in each case extracted from the actual producer, the labourer.

Since, on the one hand, the value of this labour-power determines the necessary portion of the working day; and since, on the other hand, the surplus-value is determined by the surplus portion of the working day, it follows that surplus-value bears the same ratio to variable capital, that surplus-labour does to necessary labour, or in other words, the rate of surplus-value s/v = surplus labour/necessary labour. Both ratios s/v and surplus labour/necessary labour express the same thing in different ways; in the one case by reference to materialised, incorporated labour, in the other by reference to living, fluent labour.

The rate of surplus-value is therefore an exact expression for the degree of exploitation of labour-power by capital, or of the labourer by the capitalist.

The method of calculating the rate of surplus-value is therefore, shortly, as follows.

We take the total value of the product and put the constant capital which merely re-appears in it equal to zero. What remains is the only value that has, in the process of producing the commodity, been actually created. If the amount of surplus-value be given, we have only to deduct it from this remainder, to find the variable capital. And vice versa, if the latter be given, and we require to find the surplus-value. If both be given, we have only to perform the concluding operation, viz., to calculate s/v the ratio of the surplus-value to the variable capital.

An example shows us how the capitalist converts money into capital. The product of a working day of 12 hours is 20lbs. of yarn, having a value of 30s. No less than 8/10 of this value, or 24s., is due to mere reappearance in it of the value of the means of production (20lbs. of cotton, value 20s., and spindle worn away, 4s): it is therefore constant capital. The remaining 2/10 or 6s is the new value created during the spinning process: of this one half replaces the value of the day's labour-power, or the variable capital, the remaining half constitutes a surplus-value of 3s. The total value then of the 20lbs. of yarn is made up as follows: 30s value of yarn = 24 const. + 3s var. + 3s. surpl. Since the whole of the value is contained in the 20lbs. of yarn produced, it follows that the various component parts of this value, can be represented as being contained respectively in corresponding parts of the product.

Since 12 working hours of the spinner are embodied in 6s., it follows that in yarn of the value of 30s., there must be embodied 60 working hours. And this quantity of labour-time does in fact exist in the 20lbs. of yarn; for in 8/10 or 16 lbs. there are materialised the 48 hours of labour expended, before the commencement of the spinning process, on the means of production; and in the remaining 2/10 or 4 lbs. there are materialised the 12 hours' work done during the process itself.

On a former page we saw that the value of the yarn is equal to the sum of the new value created during the production of that yarn plus the value previously existing in the means of production. It has now been shown how the various component parts of the value of the product, parts that differ functionally from each other, may be represented by corresponding proportional parts of the product itself.

To split up in this manner the product into different parts, of which one represents only the labour previously spent on the means of production, or the constant capital, another only the necessary labour spent during the process of production, or the variable capital, and another and last part only the surplus-labour expended during the same process, or the surplus-value; to do this, is, as will be seen later on from its application to complicated and hitherto unsolved problems, no less important than it is simple.

The portion of the product that represents the surplus-value, we call "surplus-produce". Since the production of surplus-value is the chief end and aim of capitalist production, it is clear that the greatness of a man's or a nation's wealth should be measured, not by the absolute quantity produced, but by the relative magnitude of the surplus-produce.

Chapter Ten: The Working Day

The limits of the working day

The sum of the necessary labour and the surplus-labour, i.e., of the periods of time during which the workman replaces the value of his labour-power, and produces the surplus-value, this sum constitutes the actual time during which he works, i.e., the working day. The working day is not a constant, but a variable quantity. One of its parts, certainly, is determined by the working time required for the reproduction of the labour-power of the labourer himself. But its total amount varies with the duration of the surplus-labour. The working day is, therefore, determinable, but is, per se, indeterminate.

The minimum limit is, however, not determinable. On the other hand, the working day has a maximum limit. It cannot be prolonged beyond a certain point. Within the twenty four hours of the natural day a man can expend only a definite quantity of his vital force. During part of the day this force must rest, sleep; during another part the man has to satisfy other physical needs. Besides these purely physical limitations, the extension of the working day encounters moral ones. The labourer needs time for satisfying his intellectual and social wants, the extent and number of which are conditioned by the general state of social advancement. The variation of the working day fluctuates, therefore, within physical and social bounds. But both these limiting conditions are of a very elastic nature, and allow the greatest latitude.

The capitalist has bought the labour-power at its day rate. To him its use-value belongs during one working day. He has thus acquired the right to make the labourer work for him during one day. But what is a working day?

The capitalist has his own views of the necessary limit of the working day. As capitalist, he is only capital personified. His soul is the soul of capital. But capital has one single life impulse, the tendency to create value and surplus-value, to make its constant factor, the means of production, absorb the greatest possible amount of surplus-labour. Capital is dead labour that, vampire-like, only lives by sucking living labour, and lives the more, the more labour it sucks. The time during which the labourer works is the time during which the capitalist consumes the labour-power he has purchased of him. If the labourer consumes his disposable time for himself, he robs the capitalist. The capitalist then takes his stand on the law of the exchange of commodities. He, like all other buyers, seeks to get the greatest possible benefit out of the use-value of his commodity.

Suddenly the voice of the labourer rises: The commodity that I have sold to you differs from the crowd of other commodities, in that its use creates value, and a value greater than its own. That is why you bought it. That which on your side appears a spontaneous expansion of capital, is on mine extra expenditure of labour-power. You and I know on the market only one law, that of the exchange of commodities. And the consumption of the commodity belongs not to the seller, but to the buyer. To you, therefore, belongs the use of my daily labour-power. But by means of the price that you pay for it each day, I must be able to reproduce it daily, and to sell it again. I will, like a sensible saving owner, husband my sole wealth, labour-power, and abstain from all foolish waste of it. I will each day spend, set in motion, put into action only as much of it as is compatible with its normal duration, and healthy development. By an unlimited extension of the working day, you may in one day use up a quantity of labour-power greater than I can restore in three. What you gain in labour I lose in substance. The use of my labour-power and the spoliation of it are quite different things. If the average time that (doing a reasonable amount of work) an average labourer can live is 30 years, the value of my labour-power which you pay me from day to day is $1/365 \times 30$ or $1/10950$ of its total value. But if you consume it in 10 years, you pay me daily $1/10950$ instead of $1/3650$ of its total value, i.e., only $1/3$ of its daily value, and you rob me, therefore, every day of $2/3$ of the value of my commodity. You pay me for one day's labour-power, whilst you use that of three days. That is against our contract and the law of exchanges. I demand, therefore, a working day of normal length, and I demand it without any appeal to your heart. You may be a model citizen; but the thing that you represent face to face with me has no heart in its breast.

We see then, that, apart from extremely elastic bounds, the nature of the exchange of commodities itself imposes no limit to the working day, no limit to surplus-labour. The capitalist maintains his rights as a purchaser when he tries to make the working day as long as possible, and to make, whenever possible, two working days out of one. On the other hand, the peculiar nature of the commodity sold implies a limit to its consumption by the purchaser, and the labourer maintains his right as seller when he wishes to reduce the working day to one of definite normal duration. There is here, therefore, an antinomy, right against right, both equally bearing the seal of the law of exchanges. Between equal rights force decides. Hence is it that in the history of capitalist production, the determination of what is a working day presents itself as the result of a struggle, a struggle between collective capital, i.e., the class of capitalists, and collective labour, i.e., the working class.

Greed for surplus labour

Capital has not invented surplus-labour. Wherever a part of society possesses the monopoly of the means of production, the labourer, free or not free, must add to the working time necessary for his own maintenance an extra working time in order to produce the means of subsistence for the owners of the means of production whether this proprietor be the Athenian nobleman, Etruscan theocrat, civis Romanus, Norman baron, American slave owner, Wallachian Boyard, modern landlord or capitalist. Hence in antiquity overwork becomes horrible only when the object is to obtain exchange value in its specific independent money-form; in the production of gold and silver. Compulsory working to death is here the recognised form of overwork.

But as soon as people, whose production still moves within the lower forms of slave-labour, corvee-labour, etc., are drawn into the whirlpool of an international market dominated by the capitalistic mode of production, the sale of their products for export becoming their principal interest, the civilised horrors of overwork are grafted on the barbaric horrors of slavery, serfdom, etc. Hence the negro labour in the Southern States of the American Union preserved something of a patriarchal character, so long as production was chiefly directed to immediate local consumption. But in proportion, as the export of cotton became of vital interest to these states, the over-working of the negro and sometimes the using up of his life in seven years of labour became a factor in a calculated and calculating system. Nothing is from this point of view more characteristic than the designation of the workers who work full time as "full-timers" and the children under 13 who are only allowed to work six hours as "half-timers". The worker is here nothing more than personified labour-time. All individual distinctions are merged in those of "full-timers" and "half-timers". To appropriate labour during all the 24 hours of the day is the inherent tendency of capitalist production.

"What is a working day? What is the length of time during which capital may consume the labour-power whose daily value it buys? How far may the working day be extended beyond the working time necessary for the reproduction of labour-power itself?" It has been seen that to these questions capital replies: the working day contains the full 24 hours, with the deduction of the few hours of repose without which labour-power absolutely refuses its services again. Hence it is self-evident that the labourer is nothing else, his whole life through, than labour-power, that therefore all his disposable time is by nature and law labour-time, to be devoted to the self-expansion of capital. Time for education, for intellectual development, for the fulfilling of social functions and for social intercourse, for the freeplay of his bodily and mental activity, even the rest time of Sunday (and that in a country of Sabbatarians!) — moonshine!

In its blind unrestrainable passion, its werewolf hunger for surplus-labour, capital oversteps not only the moral, but even the merely physical maximum bounds of the working day. It usurps the time for growth, development, and healthy maintenance of the body. It steals the time required for the consumption of fresh air and sunlight. It higgles over a meal-time, incorporating it where possible with the process of production itself, so that food is given to the labourer as to a mere means of production, as coal is supplied to the boiler, grease and oil to the machinery. It reduces the sound sleep needed for the restoration, reparation, refreshment of the bodily powers to just so many hours of torpor as the revival of an organism, absolutely exhausted, renders essential. It is not the normal maintenance of the labour-power which is to determine the limits of the working day; it is the greatest possible daily expenditure of labour-power, no matter how diseased, compulsory and painful it may be, which is to determine the limits of the labourers' period of repose. Capital cares nothing for the length of life of labour-power. All that concerns it is simply and solely the maximum of labour-power, that can be rendered fluent in a working day. It attains this end by shortening the extent of the labourer's life, as a greedy farmer snatches increased produce from the soil by robbing it of its fertility. The capitalistic mode of production (essentially the production of surplus-value, the absorption of surplus-labour) produces thus, with the extension of the working day, not only the deterioration of human labour-power by robbing it of its normal, moral, and physical conditions of development and function. It produces also the premature exhaustion and death of this labour-power itself. It extends the labourer's time of production during a given period by shortening his actual lifetime.

It takes centuries ere the "free" labourer, thanks to the development of capitalistic production, agrees, i.e., is compelled by social conditions, to sell the whole of his active life, his very capacity for work, for the price of the necessaries of life, his birthright for a mess of pottage. Hence it is natural that the lengthening of the working day, which capital, from the middle of the 14th to the end of the 17th century, tries to impose by State measures on adult labourers, approximately coincides with the shortening of the working day which, in the second half of the 19th century, has here and there been effected by the State to prevent the coining of children's blood into capital.

Centuries of struggle

The establishment of a normal working day is the result of centuries of struggle between capitalist and labourer.

The first "Statute of Labourers" (23 Edward III, 1349) found its immediate pretext (not its cause) in the great plague that decimated the people, so that, as a Tory writer says, "The difficulty of getting men to work on reasonable terms grew to such a height as to be quite intolerable". Reasonable wages were, therefore, fixed by law as well as the limits of the working day. After capital had taken centuries in extending the working day to its normal maximum limit, and then beyond this to the limit of the natural day of 12 hours, there followed, on the birth of machinism and modern industry in the last third of the 18th century, a violent encroachment like that of an avalanche in its intensity and extent. All bounds of morals and nature, age and sex, day and night, were broken down. Capital celebrated its orgies.

As soon as the working class, stunned at first by the noise and turmoil of the new system of production, recovered, in some measure, its senses, its resistance began, and first in the native land of machinism, in England. For 30 years, however, the concessions conquered by the workpeople were purely nominal. Parliament passed five Labour Laws between 1802 and 1833, but was shrewd enough not to vote a penny for their carrying out, for the requisite officials, etc. They remained a dead letter. "The fact is that prior to the Act of 1833, young persons and children were worked all night, all day, or both ad libitum."

A normal working day for modern industry only dates from the Factory Act of 1833. Nothing is more characteristic of the spirit of capital than the history of the English Factory Acts from 1833 to 1864!

The Act of 1833 declares the ordinary factory working day to be from half-past five in the morning to half past eight in the evening, and within these limits, a period of 15 hours, it is lawful to employ young persons between 13 and 18 years of age, at any time of the day, provided no one individual young person should work more than 12 hours in any one day, except in certain cases especially provided for.

The law-makers were so far from wishing to trench on the freedom of capital to exploit adult labour-power, or, as they called it, "the freedom of labour", that they created a special system in order to prevent the Factory Acts from having a consequence so outrageous. "The great evil of the factory system as at present conducted," says the first report of the Central Board of the Commission of June 28th, 1833, "has appeared to us to be that it entails the necessity of continuing the labour of children to the utmost length of that of the adults. The only remedy for this evil, short of the limitation of the labour of adults, which would, in our opinion, create an evil greater than that which is sought to be remedied, appears to be the plan of working double sets of children."... Under the name of System of Relays, this "plan" was therefore carried out.

Child labour

In order to reward the manufacturers for having, in the most barefaced way, ignored all the Acts as to children's labour passed during the last 22 years, Parliament decreed that after March 1st, 1834, no child under 11, after March 1st, 1835, no child under 12, and after March 1st, 1836, no child under 13, was to work more than eight hours in a factory. That same "reformed" Parliament, which in its delicate consideration for the manufacturers, condemned children under 13, for years to come, to 72 hours of work per week in the Factory Hell, on the other hand, forbade the planters, from the outset, to work any negro slave more than 45 hours a week.

The years 1846-47 are epoch-making in the economic history of England. The Repeal of the Corn Laws, and of the duties on cotton and other raw material; free trade proclaimed as the guiding star of legislation; in accord, the arrival of the millennium. On the other hand, in the same years, the Chartist movement and the 10 hours' agitation reached their highest point. The Ten Hours' Act came into force May 1st, 1848. To understand we must remember that none of the Factory Acts of 1833, 1844, and 1847 limited the working day of the male worker over 18, and that since 1833 the 15 hours from 5.30 a.m. to 8.30 p.m. had remained the legal "day", within the limits of which at first the 12 and later the 10 hours' labour of young persons and women had to be performed under the prescribed conditions.

The passion of capital for an unlimited and reckless extension of the working day, is first gratified in the industries earliest revolutionised by water-power, steam, and machinery: cotton, wool, flax, and silk spinning, and weaving. The changes in the material mode of production, and the corresponding changes in the social relations of the producers gave rise first to an extravagance beyond all bounds, and then in opposition to this, called forth a control on the part of Society which legally limits, regulates and makes uniform the working day and its pauses. This control appears, therefore, during the first half of the 19th century simply as exceptional legislation.

The history of the regulation of the working day in certain branches of production, and the struggle still going on in others in regard to this regulation, prove conclusively that the isolated labourer, the labourer as "free" vendor of his labour-power, when capitalist production has once attained a certain stage, succumbs without any power of resistance. The creation of a normal working day is, therefore, the product of a protracted civil war, more or less dissembled, between the capitalist class and the working class. The English factory workers were the champions, not only of the English, but of the modern working class generally, as their theorists were the first to throw down the gauntlet to the theory of capital. France limps slowly behind England. The February revolution was necessary to bring into the world the 12 hours' law, which is much more deficient than its English original. For all that, the French revolutionary method has its special advantages.

In the United States of North America every independent movement of the workers was paralysed so long as slavery disfigured a part of the Republic. Labour cannot emancipate itself in the white skin where in the black it is branded. But out of the death of slavery a new life at once arose. The first fruit of the Civil War was the eight hours' agitation, that ran with the seven-leagued boots of the locomotive from the Atlantic to the Pacific, from New England to California. For "protection" against "the serpent of their agonies", the labourers must put their heads together, and, as a class, compel the passing of a law, an all-powerful social barrier that shall prevent the very workers from selling, by voluntary contract with capital, themselves and their families into slavery and death. In place of the pompous catalogue of the "inalienable rights of man" comes the modest Magna Charta of a legally limited working day.

Chapter Eleven: Rate and Mass of Surplus-Value

With the rate there is given at the same time the mass of the surplus-value that the individual labourer furnishes to the capitalist in a definite period of time. If, e.g., the necessary labour amounts to 6 hours daily, expressed in a quantum of gold = 3 shillings, then 3s. is the daily value of one labour-power or the value of the capital advanced in the buying of one labour-power. If, further, the rate of surplus-value be = 100%, this variable capital of 3s. produces a mass of surplus-value of 3s., or the labourer supplies daily a mass of surplus-labour equal to 6 hours.

The mass of the surplus-value produced is equal to the amount of the variable capital advanced, multiplied by the rate of surplus-value; in other words: it is determined by the compound ratio between the number of labour-powers exploited simultaneously by the same capitalist and the degree of exploitation of each individual labour-power.

In the production of a definite mass of surplus-value, the decrease of one factor may be compensated by the increase of the other. Diminution of the variable capital may therefore be compensated by a proportionate rise in the degree of exploitation of labour-power, or the decrease in the number of the labourers employed by a proportionate extension of the working day. Within certain limits therefore the supply of labour exploitable by capital is independent of the supply of labourers. On the contrary, a fall in the rate of surplus-value leaves unaltered the mass of the surplus-value produced, if the amount of the variable capital, or number of the labourers employed, increases in the same proportion.

Nevertheless, the compensation of a decrease in the number of labourers employed, or of the amount of variable capital advanced, by a rise in the rate of surplus-value, or by the lengthening of the working day, has impassable limits. The absolute limit of the average working day — this being by Nature always less than 24 hours — sets an absolute limit to the compensation of a reduction of variable capital by a higher rate of surplus-value, or of the decrease of the number of labourers exploited by a higher degree of exploitation of labour-power.

The masses of value and of surplus-value produced by different capitals — the value of labour-power being given and its degree of exploitation being equal — vary directly as the amounts of the variable constituents of these capitals, i.e., as their constituents transformed into living labour-power.

Not every sum of money, or of value, is at pleasure transformable into capital. To effect this transformation, in fact, a certain minimum of money or of exchange-value must be presupposed in the hands of the individual possessor of money or commodities. The minimum of variable capital is the cost price of a single labour-power, employed day in, day out, for the production of surplus-value. If this labourer were in possession of his own means of production, and were satisfied to live as a labourer, he need not work beyond the time necessary for the reproduction of his means of subsistence, say 8 hours a day. He would, besides, only require the means of production sufficient for 8 working hours. The capitalist, on the other hand, who makes him do, besides these 8 hours, say 4 hours' surplus-labour, requires an additional sum of money for furnishing the additional means of production. On our supposition, however, he would have to employ two labourers in order to live, on the surplus-value appropriated daily, as well as, and no better than a labourer, i.e., to be able to satisfy his necessary wants. In this case the mere maintenance of life would be the end of his production, not the increase of wealth; but this latter is implied in capitalist production. That he may live only twice as well as an ordinary labourer, and besides turn half of the surplus-value into capital, he would have to raise, with the number of labourers, the minimum of the capital advanced ~ times. Of course he can take to work himself, participate directly in the process of production, but he is then only a hybrid between capitalist and labourer, a "small master." A certain stage of production necessitates that the capitalist be able to devote the whole of the time during which he functions as a capitalist, i.e., as personified capital, to the appropriation and therefore control of the labour of others, and to the selling of the products of this labour.

Within the process of production, as we have seen, capital acquired the command over labour. The capitalist takes care that the labourer does his work regularly and with the proper degree of intensity. Capital further developed into a coercive relation, which compels the working class to do more work than the narrow round of its own life-wants prescribes. As a producer of the activity of others, as a pumper-out of surplus-labour and exploiter of labour-power, it surpasses in energy, disregard of bounds, recklessness and efficiency, all earlier systems of production based on directly compulsory labour.

It is now no longer the labourer that employs the means of production, but the means of production that employ the labourer. Instead of being consumed by him as material elements of his productive activity, they consume him as the ferment necessary to their own life-process, and the life-process of capital consists only in its movement as value constantly expanding, constantly multiplying itself.

Part 4
Production of Relative Surplus-Value
Chapter Twelve: The Concept of Relative Surplus-Value

Hitherto in treating of surplus-value, arising from a simple prolongation of the working day, we have assumed the mode of production to be given and invariable. But when surplus-value has to be produced by the conversion of necessary labour into surplus-labour, it by no means suffices for capital to take over the labour-process in the form under which it has been historically handed down, and then simply to prolong the duration of that process. The technical and social conditions of the process, and consequently the very mode of production must be revolutionised, before the productiveness of labour can be increased. By that means alone can the value of labour-power be made to sink, and the portion of the working day necessary for the reproduction of that value, be shortened.

The surplus-value produced by prolongation of the working day, I call absolute surplus-value. On the other hand, the surplus-value arising from the curtailment of the necessary labour-time, and from the corresponding alteration in the respective lengths of the two components of the working day, I call relative surplus-value.

The shortening of the working day is by no means what is aimed at, in capitalist production, when labour is economised by increasing its productiveness. It is only the shortening of the labour-time, necessary for the production of a definite quantity of commodities, that is aimed at.

The capitalist who applies the improved method of production appropriates to surplus-labour a greater portion of the working day, than the other capitalists in the same trade. On the other hand, however, this extra surplus-value vanishes, so soon as the new method of production has become general and has consequently caused the difference between the individual value of the cheapened commodity and its social value to vanish.

The law of the determination of value by labour-time, a law which brings under its sway the individual capitalist who applies the new method of production, by compelling him to sell his goods under their social value, this same law, acting as a coercive law of competition, forces his competitors to adopt the new method.

In order to effect a fall in the value of labour-power, the increase in the productiveness of labour must seize upon those branches of industry, whose products determine the value of labour-power, and consequently either belong to the class of customary means of subsistence, or are capable of supplying the place of those means.

The value of commodities is in inverse ratio to the productiveness of labour. And so, too, is the value of labour-power, because it depends on the values of commodities. Relative surplus-value is, on the contrary, directly proportional to that productiveness. The cheapened commodity, of course, causes only a pro tanto fall in the value of labour-power, a fall proportional to the extent of that commodity's employment in the reproduction of labour-power.

Chapter Thirteen: Co-operation

A greater number of labourers working together, at the same time, in one place (or, if you will, in the same field of labour), in order to produce the same sort of commodity under the mastership of one capitalist, constitutes, both historically and logically, the starting point of capitalist production.

When numerous labourers work together side by side, whether in one and the same process, or in different but connected processes, they are said to co-operate, or to work in co-operation.

In every industry, each individual labourer, be he Peter or Paul, differs from the average labourer. These individual differences, or "errors" as they are called in mathematics, compensate one another, and vanish, whenever a certain minimum number of workmen are employed together.

Even without an alteration in the system of working, the simultaneous employment of a large number of labourers effects a revolution in the material conditions of the labour-process. The buildings in which they work, the store-houses for the raw material, the implements and utensils used simultaneously or in turns by the workmen; in short, a portion of the means of production are now consumed in common. On the one hand, the exchange-value of these means of production is not increased; for the exchange-value of a commodity is not raised by its use-value being consumed more thoroughly and to greater advantage. On the other hand, they are used in common, and therefore on a larger scale than before. A room where twenty weavers work at twenty looms must be larger than the room of a single weaver with two assistants. But it costs less labour to build one workshop for twenty persons than to build ten to accommodate two weavers each; thus the value of the means of production that are concentrated for use in common on a large scale does not increase in direct proportion to the expansion and to the increased useful effect of those means. When consumed in common, they give up a smaller part of their value to each single product. Owing to this, the value of a part of the constant capital falls, and in proportion to the magnitude of the fall, the total value of the commodity also falls. The effect is the same as if the means of production had cost less.

Just as the offensive power of a squadron of cavalry, or the defensive power of a regiment of infantry, is essentially different from the sum of the offensive or defensive powers of the individual cavalry or infantry soldiers taken separately, so the sum total of the mechanical forces exerted by isolated workmen differs from the social force that is developed, when many hands take part simultaneously in one and the same undivided operation.

Not only have we here an increase in the productive power of the individual, by means of co-operation, but the creation of a new power, namely, the collective power of masses.

Apart from the new power that arises from the fusion of many forces into one single force, mere social contact begets in most industries an emulation and a stimulation of the animal spirits that heighten the efficiency of each individual workman. Hence it is that a dozen persons working together will, in their collective working day of 144 hours, produce far more than twelve isolated men each working twelve hours, or than one man who works twelve days in succession. The reason of this is that a man is, if not as Aristotle contends, a political, at all events a social animal.

Although a number of men may be occupied together at the same time on the same or the same kind of work, yet the labour of each, as a part of the collective labour, may correspond to a distinct phase of the labour-process, through all whose phases, in consequence of co-operation, the subject of their labour passes with greater speed.

For instance, if a dozen masons place themselves in a row, so as to pass stones from the foot of a ladder to its summit, each of them does the same thing; nevertheless, their separate acts form connected parts of one total operation; they are particular phases, which must be gone through by each stone; and the stones are thus carried up quicker by the 24 hands of the row of them than they could be if each man went separately up and down the ladder with his burden. The object is carried over the same distance in a shorter time. Again, a combination of labour occurs whenever a building, for instance, is taken in hand on different sides simultaneously; although here also the co-operating masons are doing the same or the same kind of work.

If the work be complicated, then the mere number of the men who co-operate allows of the various operations being apportioned to different hands, and, consequently, of being carried on simultaneously. The time necessary for the completion of the whole work is thereby shortened.

On the one hand, co-operation allows of the work being carried on over an extended space; it is consequently imperatively called for in certain undertakings. On the other hand, while extending the scale of production, it renders possible a relative contraction of the arena, whereby a number of useless expenses are cut down.

The number of the labourers that co-operate, or the scale of co-operation, depends, in the first instance, on the amount of capital that the individual capitalist can spare for the purchase of labour-power; in other words, on the extent to which a single capitalist has command over the means of subsistence of a number of labourers. And as with the variable, so it is with the constant capital. Hence, concentration of large masses of the means of production in the hands of individual capitalists, is a material condition for the co-operation of wage-labourers, and the extent of the co-operation or the scale of production, depends on the extent of this concentration.

That a capitalist should command on the field of production, is now as indispensable as that a general should command on the field of battle. All combined labour on a large scale requires, more or less, a directing authority, in order to secure the harmonious working of the individual activities, and to perform the general functions that have their origin in the action of the combined organism, as distinguished from the action of its separate organs. A single violin player is his own conductor; an orchestra requires a separate one.

The work of directing, superintending, and adjusting becomes one of the functions of capital, from the moment that the labour under the control of capital becomes co-operative Once a function of capital, it acquires special characteristics.

When the labourer co-operates systematically with others, he strips off the fetters of his individuality, and develops the capabilities of his species.

The connection existing between their various labours appears to them, ideally, in the shape of a preconceived plan of the capitalist, and practically in the shape of the authority of the same capitalist, in the shape of the powerful will of another, who subjects their activity to his aims.

As the number of the co-operating labourers increases, so too does their resistance to the domination of capital, and with it, the necessity for capital to overcome this resistance by counter-pressure. The control exercised by the capitalist is not only a special function, due to the nature of the social labour-process, and peculiar to that process, but it is, at the same time, a function of the exploitation of a social labour-process, and is consequently rooted in the unavoidable antagonism between the exploiter and the living and labouring raw material he exploits.

If the control of the capitalist is in substance twofold by reason of the twofold nature of the process of production itself, in form that control is despotic. So soon as capital has reached that minimum amount with which capitalist production as such begins, he hands over the work of direct and constant supervision of the individual workmen, and groups of workmen, to a special kind of wage labourer. An industrial army of workmen requires, like a real army, officers (managers), and sergeants (foremen, overlookers) who, while the work is being done, command in the name of the capitalist. It is not because he is a leader of industry that a man is a capitalist; on the contrary, he is a leader of industry because he is a capitalist. The leadership of industry is an attribute of capital, just as in feudal times the functions of general and judge were attributes of landed property.

The productive power developed by the labourer when working in co-operation, is the productive power of capital. This power is developed gratuitously, whenever the workmen are placed under given conditions, and it is capital that places them under such conditions. Because this power costs capital nothing, and because, on the other hand, the labourer himself does not develop it before his labour belongs to capital, it appears as a power with which capital is endowed by Nature — a productive power that is immanent in capital. Co-operation, such as we find it at the dawn of human development, is based, on the one hand, on ownership in common of the means of production, and on the other hand, on the fact that, in those cases, each individual has no more torn himself off from the navel-string of his tribe or community, than each bee has freed itself from connection with the hive. Such co-operation is distinguished from capitalistic co-operation by both of the above characteristics. The sporadic application of co-operation on a large scale in ancient times, in the Middle Ages, and in modern colonies, reposes on relations of dominion and servitude, principally on slavery. The capitalistic form, on the contrary, presupposes from first to last the free wage labourer, who sells his labour-power to capital. Historically, however, this form is developed in opposition to peasant agriculture and to the carrying on of independent handicrafts. From the standpoint of these, capitalistic co-operation does not manifest itself as a particular historical form of co-operation, but co-operation itself appears to be a historical form peculiar to, and specifically distinguishing, the capitalist process of production.

Co-operation is the first change experienced by the actual labour-process, when subjected to capital. This change takes place spontaneously. The simultaneous employment of a large number of wage-labourers, in one and the same process, forms the starting point of capitalist production, and is a necessary concomitant.

Chapter Fourteen: Division of Labour and Manufacture

That co-operation which is based on division of labour assumes its typical form in manufacture, and is the prevalent characteristic form of the capitalist process of production throughout the manufacturing period properly so called. That period, roughly speaking, extends from the middle of the 16th to the last third of the 18th century.

Manufacture takes its rise in two ways: by the assemblage, in one workshop under the control of a single capitalist, of labourers belonging to various independent handicrafts, but through whose hands a given article must pass on its way to completion. As an example of that kind we may take a watch. Formerly the individual work of an artificer, the watch has been transformed into the social product of an immense number of detail labourers, and all these come together for the first time in the hand that binds them into one mechanical whole.

Manufacture also arises in a way exactly the reverse of this — namely, by one capitalist employing simultaneously in one workshop a number of artificers, who all do the same or the same kind of work. The work is redistributed. Instead of each man being allowed to perform all the various operations in succession, these operations are changed into disconnected, isolated ones, carried on side by side; each is assigned to a different artificer, and the whole of them together are performed simultaneously by the co-operating workmen. The commodity, from being the individual product of an independent artificer, becomes the social product of a union of artificers. This perfected form produces articles that go through connected phases of development, through a series of processes step by step, like the wire in the manufacture of needles, which passes through the hands of 72 and sometimes even 92 different detail workmen.

The mode in which manufacture arises, its growth out of handicrafts, is therefore twofold. On the one hand, it arises from the union of various independent handicrafts, which become stripped of their independence and specialised to such an extent as to be reduced to mere supplementary partial processes in the production of one particular commodity. On the other hand, it arises from the co-operation of artificers of one handicraft; it splits up that particular handicraft into its various detail operations, isolating, and making these operations independent of one another up to the point where each becomes the exclusive function of a particular labourer. On the one hand, therefore, manufacture either introduces division of labour into a process of production, or further develops that division; on the other hand, it unites together handicrafts that were formerly separate. But whatever may have been its particular starting point, its final form is invariably the same — a productive mechanism whose parts are human beings.

Whether complex or simple, each operation has to be done by hand, retains the character of a handicraft, and is therefore dependent on the strength, skill, quickness, and sureness of the individual workman in handling his tools. The handicraft continues to be the basis. This narrow technical basis excludes a really scientific analysis of any definite process of industrial production, since it is still a condition that each detail process gone through by the product must be capable of being done by hand and of forming, in its way, a separate handicraft. It is just because handicraft skill continues, in this way, to be the foundation of the process of production, that each workman becomes exclusively assigned to a partial function, and that for the rest of his life, his labour-power is turned into the organ of this detail function.

It is clear that a labourer who all his life performs one and the same simple operation, converts his whole body into the automatic, specialised implement of that operation. Consequently, he takes less time in doing it, than the artificer who performs a whole series of operations in succession. But the collective labourer is made up solely of such specialised detail labourers. Hence, in comparison with the independent handicraft, more is produced in a given time, or the productive power of labour is increased.

Moreover, when once this fractional work is established as the exclusive function of one person, the methods it employs become perfected. The workman's continued repetition of the same simple act, and the concentration of his attention on it, teach him by experience how to attain the desired effect with the minimum of exertion. But since there are always several generations of labourers living at one time, and working together at the manufacture of a given article, the technical skill, the tricks of the trade thus acquired, become established, and are accumulated and handed down.

Manufacture, in fact, produces the skill of the detail labourer, by reproducing, and systematically driving to an extreme within the workshop, the naturally developed differentiation of trades, which it found ready to hand in society at large. On the other hand, the conversion of fractional work into the life-calling of one man corresponds to the tendency shown by earlier societies to make trades hereditary; either to petrify them into castes, or whenever definite historical conditions beget in the individual a tendency to vary in a manner incompatible with the nature of castes, to ossify them into guilds.

An artificer, who performs one after another the various fractional operations in the production of a finished article, must at one time change his place, at another his tools. The transition from one operation to another interrupts the flow of his labour, and creates, so to say, gaps in his working day. These gaps close up so soon as he is tied to one and the same operation all day long; they vanish in proportion as the changes in his work diminish. The resulting increased productive power is owing either to an increased expenditure of labour-power in a given time — i.e., to increased intensity of labour — or to a decrease in the amount of labour-power unproductively consumed.

The productiveness of labour depends not only on the proficiency of the workman, but on the perfection of his tools. Alterations become necessary in the implements that previously served more than one purpose. The direction taken by this change is determined by the difficulties experienced in consequence of the unchanged form of the implement. Manufacture is characterised by the differentiation of the instruments of labour — a differentiation whereby implements of a given sort acquire fixed shapes, adapted to each particular application, and by the specialisation of those instruments, giving to each special instrument its full play only in the hands of a specific detail labourer.

In so far as a manufacture, when first started, combines scattered handicrafts, it lessens the space by which the various phases of production are separated from each other. The time taken in passing from one stage to another is shortened, so is the labour that effectuates this passage. In comparison with a handicraft, productive power is gained. On the other hand, division of labour, which is the principle of manufacture, requires the isolation of the various stages of production and their independence of each other. The establishment and maintenance of a connexion between the isolated functions necessitates the incessant transport of the article from one hand to another, and from one process to another. From the standpoint of modern mechanical industry, this necessity stands forth as a characteristic and costly disadvantage, and one that is immanent in the principle of manufacture.

Since the fractional product of each detail labourer is, at the same time, only a particular stage in the development of one and the same finished article, each labourer, or each group of labourers, prepares the raw material for another labourer or group. The result of the labour of the one is the starting point for the labour of the other. The one workman therefore gives occupation directly to the other. The labour-time necessary in each partial process, for attaining the desired effect, is learnt by experience; and the mechanism of Manufacture, as a whole, is based on the assumption that a given result will be obtained in a given time. It is only on this assumption that the various supplementary labour-processes can proceed uninterruptedly, simultaneously, and side by side.

This direct dependence of the operations, and therefore of the labourers, on each other, compels each one of them to spend on his work no more than the necessary time, and thus a continuity, uniformity, regularity, order, and even intensity of labour, of quite a different kind, is begotten than is to be found in an independent handicraft or even in simple co-operation. The rule that the labour-time expended on a commodity should not exceed that which is socially necessary for its production, appears, in the production of commodities generally, to be established by the mere effect of competition; since, to express ourselves superficially, each single producer is obliged to sell his commodity at its market price. In Manufacture, on the contrary, the turning out of a given quantum of product in a given time is a technical law of the process of production itself.

The division of labour, as carried out in Manufacture, not only simplifies and multiplies the qualitatively different parts of the social collective labourer, but also creates a fixed mathematical relation or ratio which regulates the quantitative extent of those parts — i.e., the relative number of labourers, or the relative size of the group of labourers, for each detail operation. It develops, along with the qualitative sub-division of the social labour process, a quantitative rule and proportionality for that process.

Early in the manufacturing period, the principle of lessening the necessary labour-time in the production of commodities was accepted and formulated: and the use of machines, especially for certain simple first processes that have to be conducted on a very large scale, and with the application of great force, sprang up here and there. But, on the whole, machinery played that subordinate part which Adam Smith assigns to it in comparison with division of labour.

The collective labourer, formed by the combination of a number of detail labourers, is the mechanism specially characteristic of the manufacturing period. The various operations that are performed in turns by the producer of a commodity, and coalesce one with another during the progress of production, lay claim to him in various ways. In one operation he must exert more strength, in another more skill, in another more attention; and the same individual does not possess all these qualities in an equal degree. After Manufacture has once separated, made independent, and isolated the various operations, the labourers are divided, classified, and grouped according to their predominating qualities. If their natural endowments are, on the one hand, the foundation on which the division of labour is built up, on the other hand, Manufacture, once introduced, develops in them new powers that are by nature fitted only for limited and special functions. The collective labourer now possesses, in an equal degree of excellence, all the qualities requisite for production, and expends them in the most economical manner, by exclusively employing all his organs, consisting of particular labourers, or groups of labourers, in performing their special functions. The one-sidedness and the deficiencies of the detail labourer become perfections when he is a part of the collective labourer. The habit of doing only one thing converts him into a never-failing instrument, while his connexion with the whole mechanism compels him to work with the regularity of the parts of a machine.

Since the collective labourer has functions, both simple and complex, both high and low, his members, the individual labour-powers, require different degrees of training, and must therefore have different values. Manufacture, therefore, develops a hierarchy of labour-powers, to which there corresponds a scale of wages.

Furthermore, manufacture begets, in every handicraft that it seizes upon, a class of so-called unskilled labourers, a class which handicraft industry strictly excluded. If it develops a one-sided specialty into a perfection, at the expense of the whole of a man's working capacity, it also begins to make a specialty of the absence of all development. Alongside of the hierarchic gradation there steps the simple separation of the labourers into skilled and unskilled. For the latter, the cost of apprenticeship vanishes; for the former, it diminishes. The fall in the value of labour-power, caused by the disappearance or diminution of the expense of apprenticeship, implies a direct increase of surplus-value for the benefit of capital; for everything that shortens the necessary labour-time required for the reproduction of labour-power, extends the domain of surplus-labour. The mechanism that is made up of numerous individual detail labourers belongs to the capitalist. Hence, the productive power resulting from a combination of labourers appears to be the productive power of capital.

If, at first, the workman sells his labour-power to capital, because the material means of producing a commodity fail him, now his very labour-power refuses its services unless it has been sold to capital. Its functions can be exercised only in an environment that exists in the workshop of the capitalist after the sale. By nature unfitted to make anything independently, the manufacturing labourer develops productive activity as a mere appendage of the capitalist's workshop. As the chosen people bore in their features the sign manual of Jehovah, so division of labour brands the manufacturing workman as the property of capital.

In order to make the collective labourer, and through him capital, rich in social productive power, each labourer must be made poor in individual productive powers. As a matter of fact, some few manufacturers in the middle of the 18th century preferred, for certain operations that were trade secrets, to employ half-idiotic persons. Some crippling of body and mind is inseparable even from division of labour in society as a whole.

However, manufacture is the first to afford the materials for, and to give a start to, industrial pathology.

Division of labour in manufacture creates new conditions for the lordship of capital over labour. If, therefore, on the one hand, it presents itself historically as a progress and as a necessary phase in the economic development of society, on the other hand it is a refined and civilised method of exploitation.

Hence throughout the whole manufacturing period there runs the complaint of want of discipline among the workmen. Capital is constantly compelled to wrestle with the insubordination of the workmen. Capital failed to become the master of the whole disposable working-time of the manufacturing labourers.

Manufacture was unable either to seize upon the production of society to its full extent, or to revolutionise that production to its very core. It towered up as an economical work of art on the broad foundation of the town handicrafts, and of the rural domestic industries. At a given stage in its development, the narrow technical basis on which manufacture rested came into conflict with requirements of production that were created by manufacture itself.

One of its most finished creations was the workshop for the production of the instruments of labour themselves, including especially the complicated mechanical apparatus then already employed. This workshop, the product of the division of labour in manufacture, produced in its turn — machines.

Chapter Fifteen: Machinery and Modern Industry

In manufacture, the revolution in the mode of production begins with the labour-power, in modern industry it begins with the instruments of labour. Our first inquiry then is, how the instruments of labour are converted from tools into machines, or what is the difference between a machine and the implements of a handicraft?

All fully developed machinery consists of three essentially different parts, the motor mechanism, the transmitting mechanism, and finally the tool or working machine. The motor mechanism is that which puts the whole in motion. The transmitting mechanism regulates the motion, changes its form where necessary (as, for instance, from linear to circular) and divides and distributes it among the working machines. The tool or working machine is that part of the machinery with which the industrial revolution of the 18th century started. And to this day it constantly serves as such a starting point, whenever a handicraft, or a manufacture, is turned into an industry carried on by machinery.

On a closer examination of the working machine proper, we find in it, as a general rule, though often, no doubt, under very altered forms, the apparatus and tools used by the handicraftsman or manufacturing workman; with this difference, that instead of being human implements, they are the implements of a mechanism, or mechanical implements. Either the entire machine is only a more or less altered mechanical edition of the old handicraft tool, as, for instance, the power-loom; or the working parts fitted in the frame of the machine are old acquaintances, as spindles are in a mule, needles in a stocking-loom, saws in a sawing machine, and knives in a chopping machine. The distinction between these tools and the body proper of the machine exists from their very birth; for they continue for the most part to be produced by handicraft, or by manufacture, and are afterwards fitted into the body of the machine, which is the product of machinery. The machine proper is therefore a mechanism that, after being set in motion, performs with its tools the same operations that were formerly done by the workman with similar tools. Whether the motive power is derived from man, or from some other machine, makes no difference in this respect.

From the moment that the tool proper is taken from man, and fitted into a mechanism, a machine takes the place of a mere implement. The difference strikes one at once, even in those cases where man himself continues to be the prime mover. The number of implements that he himself can use simultaneously is limited by the number of his own natural instruments of production, by the number of his bodily organs. In Germany, they tried at first to make one spinner work two spinning wheels, that is, to work simultaneously with both hands and both feet. This was too difficult. Later, a treadle spinning wheel with two spindles was invented, but adepts in spinning, who could spin two threads at once, were almost as scarce as two-headed men.

The Jenny, on the other hand, even at its very birth, spun with 12-18 spindles, and the stocking-loom knits with many thousand needles at once. The number of tools that a machine can bring into play simultaneously, is from the very first emancipated from the organic limits that hedge in the tools of a handicraftsman. Increase in the size of the machine, and in the number of its working tools, calls for a more massive mechanism to drive it; and this mechanism requires, in order to overcome its resistance, a mightier moving power than that of man. Not till the invention of Watt's second and so-called double-acting steam-engine, was a prime mover found, that begot its own force by the consumption of coal and water, whose power was entirely under man's control, that was mobile and a means of locomotion, that was urban and not, like the water-wheel, rural, that permitted production to be concentrated in towns instead of, like the water-wheels, being scattered up and down the country, that was of universal technical application, and, relatively speaking, little affected in its choice of residence by local circumstances. The greatness of Watt's genius showed itself in the specification of the patent that he took out in April, 1784. In that specification his steam-engine is described, not as an invention for a specific purpose, but as an agent universally applicable in Mechanical Industry.

The motive mechanism grows with the number of the machines that are turned simultaneously, and the transmitting mechanism becomes a wide-spreading apparatus. We now proceed to distinguish the co-operation of a number of machines of one kind from a complex system of machinery. In the one case, the product is entirely made by a single machine. Whether this be merely a reproduction of one complicated manual implement, or a combination of various simple implements specialised by Manufacture, in either case, in the factory, we meet again with simple co-operation; and, this co-operation presents itself to us, in the first instance, as the conglomeration in one place of similar and simultaneously acting machines. A real machinery system, however, does not take the place of these independent machines, until the subject of labour goes through a connected series of detail processes, that are carried out by a chain of machines of various kinds, the one supplementing the other. Here we have again the co-operation by division of labour that characterises Manufacture; only now, it is a combination of detail machines.

The collective machine, now an organised system of various kinds of single machines, and of groups of single machines, becomes more and more perfect, the more the process as a whole becomes a continuous one, i.e., the less the raw material is interrupted in its passage from its first phase to its last; in other words, the more its passage from one phase to another is effected, not by the hand of man, but by the machinery itself. In Manufacture the isolation of each detail process is a condition imposed by the nature of division of labour, but in the fully developed factory the continuity of those processes is, on the contrary, imperative.

As soon as a machine executes, without man's help, all the movements requisite to elabourate the raw material, needing only attendance from him, we have an automatic system of machinery.

An organised system of machines, to which motion is communicated by the transmitting mechanism from a central automaton, is the most developed form of production by machinery. Here we have, in the place of the isolated machine, a mechanical monster whose body fills whole factories, and whose demon power, at first veiled under the slow and measured motions of his giant limbs, at length breaks out into the fast and furious whirl of his countless working organs.

Just as the individual machine retains a dwarfish character, so long as it is worked by the power of man alone, and just as no system of machinery could be properly developed before the steam engine took the place of the earlier motive powers; so, too, Modern Industry was crippled in its complete development, so long as its characteristic instrument of production, the machine, owed its existence to personal strength and personal skill.

Machinery operates only by means of associated labour, or labour in common. Hence, the co-operative character of the labour-process is, in the latter case, a technical necessity dictated by the instrument of labour itself. Machinery, like every other component of constant capital, creates no new value, but yields up its own value to the product that it serves to beget. Given the rate at which machinery transfers its value to the product, the amount of value so transferred depends on the total value of the machinery. The less labour it contains, the less value it imparts to the product. The less value it gives up, so much the more productive it is, and so much the more its services approximate to those of natural forces. The productiveness of a machine is therefore measured by the human labour-power it replaces.

The use of machinery for the exclusive purpose of cheapening the product, is limited in this way, that less labour must be expended in producing the machinery than is displaced by the employment of that machinery. For the capitalist, however, this use is still more limited. Instead of paying for the labour, he only pays the value of the labour-power employed; therefore, the limit to his using a machine is fixed by the difference between the value of the machine and the value of the labour-power replaced by it.

In so far as machinery dispenses with muscular power, it becomes a means of employing labourers of slight muscular strength, and those whose bodily development is incomplete, but whose limbs are all the more supple. The labour of women and children was, therefore, the first thing sought for by capitalists who used machinery.

That mighty substitute for labour and labourers was forthwith changed into a means for increasing the number of wage-labourers by enrolling, under the direct sway of capital, every member of the workman's family, without distinction of age or sex. Compulsory work for the capitalist usurped the place, not only of the children's play, but also of free labour at home within moderate limits for the support of the family.

Machinery, by throwing every member of that family on to the labour market, spreads the value of the man's labour-power over his whole family. It thus depreciates his labour-power. In order that the family may live, four people must now, not only labour, but expend surplus-labour for the capitalist. Thus we see, that machinery, while augmenting the human material that forms the principal object of capital's exploiting power, at the same time raises the degree of exploitation.

Previously, the workman sold his own labour-power, which he disposed of nominally as a free agent. Now he sells wife and child. He has become a slave dealer.

As was shown by an official medical inquiry in the year 1861, the high death-rates are, apart from local causes, principally due to the employment of the mothers away from their homes, and to the neglect and maltreatment consequent on her absence; beside this, there arises an unnatural estrangement between mother and child, and as a consequence intentional starving and poisoning of the children. In fact, the revolution in the mode of cultivation had led to the introduction of the industrial system. Married women, who work in gangs along with boys and girls, are, for a stipulated sum of money, placed at the disposal of the farmer, by a man called "the undertaker," who contracts for the whole gang. "These gangs will sometimes travel many miles from their own village; they are to be met morning and evening on the roads." Every phenomenon of the factory districts is here reproduced, including, but to a greater extent, ill-disguised infanticide, and dosing children with opiates.

The moral degradation caused by the capitalistic exploitation of women and children has been so exhaustively depicted by F Engels in his *Lage der Arbeitenden Klasse Englands*, and other writers, that I need only mention the subject in this place.

The spirit of capitalist production stands out clearly in the ludicrous wording of the so-called education clauses in the Factory Acts, in the absence of an administrative machinery, an absence that again makes the compulsion illusory, in the opposition of the manufacturers themselves to these education clauses, and in the tricks and dodges they put in practice for evading them.

If machinery be the most powerful means for increasing the productiveness of labour — i.e., for shortening the working time required in the production of a commodity, it becomes in the hands of capital the most powerful means, in those industries first invaded by it, for lengthening the working day beyond all bounds set by human nature.

The active life-time of a machine is, however, clearly dependent on the length of the working day, or on the duration of the daily labour-process multiplied by the number of days for which the process is carried on.

The material wear and tear of a machine is of two kinds. The one arises from use, as coins wear away by circulating, the other from non-use, as a sword rusts when left in its scabbard.

But in addition to the material wear and tear, a machine also undergoes what we may call a moral depreciation. It loses exchange-value, either by machines of the same sort being produced cheaper than it, or by better machines entering into competition with it. In both cases its value is determined by the labour-time requisite to reproduce either it or the better machine. It has, therefore, lost value more or less. The shorter the period taken to reproduce its total value, the less is the danger of moral depreciation; and the longer the working day, the shorter is that period. When machinery is first introduced, new methods of reproducing it more cheaply follow blow upon blow, and so do improvements, that not only affect individual parts and details of the machine, but its entire build. It is, therefore, in the early days of the life of machinery that this special incentive to the prolongation of the working day makes itself felt most acutely. The development of the factory system fixes a constantly increasing portion of the capital in a form, in which, on the one hand, its value is capable of continual self-expansion, and in which, on the other hand, it loses both use-value and exchange-value whenever it loses contact with living labour. Machinery produces relative surplus-value; not only by directly depreciating the value of labour power, and by indirectly cheapening the same through cheapening the commodities that enter into its reproduction, but also, when it is first introduced sporadically into an industry, by converting the labour employed by the owner of that machinery, into labour of a higher degree and greater efficacy, by raising the social value of the article produced above its individual value, and thus enabling the capitalist to replace the value of a day's labour-power by a smaller portion of the value of the day's product. During this transition period, when the use of machinery is a sort of monopoly, the profits are therefore exceptional.

As the use of machinery becomes more general in a particular industry, the social value of the produce sinks down to its individual value, and the law that surplus-value does not arise from the labour-power that has been replaced by the machinery, but from the labour-power actually employed in working with the machinery, asserts itself. It is impossible, for instance, to squeeze as much surplus-value out of 2 as out of 24 labourers. If each of these 24 men gives only one hour of surplus-labour in 12, the 24 men give together 24 hours of surplus-labour, while 24 hours is the total labour of the two men. Hence, the application of machinery to the production of surplus-value implies a contradiction which is immanent in it, since, of the two factors of the surplus-value created by a given amount of capital, one, the rate of surplus-value cannot be increased, except by diminishing the other, the number of workmen.

This contradiction comes to light as soon as by the general employment of machinery in a given industry, the value of the machine-produced commodity regulates the value of all commodities of the same sort; and it is this contradiction that, in its turn, drives the capitalist, without his being conscious of the fact, to excessive lengthening of the working day, in order that he may compensate the decrease in the relative number of labourers exploited, by an increase not only of the relative, but of the absolute surplus-labour.

If, then, the capitalistic employment of machinery, on the one hand, supplies new and powerful motives to an excessive lengthening of the working day, and radically changes, as well the methods of labour, as also the character of the social working organism, in such a manner as to break down all opposition to this tendency, on the other hand it produces, partly by opening out to the capitalist new strata of the working class, previously inaccessible to him, partly by setting free the labourers it supplants, a surplus working population, which is compelled to submit to the dictation of capital. Hence that remarkable phenomenon in the history of Modern Industry, that machinery sweeps away every moral and natural restriction on the length of the working day. Hence, too, the economical paradox, that the most powerful instrument for shortening labour time becomes the most unfailing means for placing every moment of the labourer's time and that of his family at the disposal of the capitalist for the purpose of expanding the value of his capital.

It is self-evident, that in proportion as the use of machinery spreads, and the experience of a special class of workmen habituated to machinery accumulates, the rapidity and intensity of labour increase as a natural consequence. Thus in England, during half a century, lengthening of the working day went hand in hand with increasing intensity of factory labour. Nevertheless a point must inevitably be reached, where extension of the working day and intensity of the labour mutually exclude one another, in such a way that lengthening of the working day becomes compatible only with a lower degree of intensity, and a higher degree of intensity only with a shortening of the working day. So soon as the revolt of the working class compelled Parliament to shorten compulsorily the hours of labour, and to begin by imposing a normal working day on factories proper, so soon as an increased production of surplus value by the prolongation of the working day was once for all put a stop to, from that moment capital threw itself with all its might into the production of relative surplus-value, by hastening on the further improvement of machinery.

At the same time a change took place in the nature of relative surplus-value. The denser hour of the ten hours' working day contains more labour, i.e., expended labour-power, than the more porous hour of the twelve hours working day. The product therefore of one of the former hours has as much or more value than has the product of the latter hours.

How is the labour intensified?

The first effect of shortening the working day results from the self-evident law, that the efficiency of labour power is in an inverse ratio to the duration of its expenditure. Hence, within certain limits what is lost by shortening the duration is gained by the increasing tension of labour-power. So soon as that shortening becomes compulsory, machinery becomes in the hands of capital the objective means, systematically employed for squeezing out more labour in a given time. This is effected in two ways: by increasing the speed of the machinery, and by giving the workman more machinery to tend.

Improved construction of the machinery is necessary, partly because without it greater pressure cannot be put on the workman, and partly because the shortened hours of labour force the capitalist to exercise the strictest watch over the cost of production. The improvements in the steam-engine have increased the piston speed, and at the same time have made it possible, by means of a greater economy of power, to drive with the same or even a smaller consumption of coal more machinery with the same engine. The improvements in the transmitting mechanism have lessened friction, have reduced the diameter and weight of the shafting to a constantly decreasing minimum. Finally, the improvements in the operative machines have, while reducing their size increased their speed and efficiency, as in the modern power-loom or, while increasing the size of their frame-work, have also increased the extent and number of their working parts, as in spinning mules, or have added to the speed of these working parts by imperceptible alterations of detail, such as the spindles in self-acting mules.

Along with the tool, the skill of the workman in handling it passes over to the machine. The capabilities of the tool are emancipated from the restraints that are inseparable from human labour-power. Thereby the technical foundation on which is based the division of labour in Manufacture is swept away. Hence, in the place of the hierarchy of specialised workmen that characterises manufacture there steps, in the automatic factory, a tendency to equalise and reduce to one and the same level every kind of work that has to be done by the minders of the machines; in the place of the artificially produced differentiations of the detail workmen, step the natural differences of age and sex.

The life-long speciality of handling one and the same tool now becomes the life-long speciality of serving one and the same machine. Machinery is put to a wrong use, with the object of transforming the workman, from his very childhood, into a part of a detail-machine. At the same time that factory work exhausts the nervous system to the uttermost, it does away with the many-sided play of the muscles, and confiscates every atom of freedom, in both bodily and intellectual activity. The lightening of the labour, even, becomes a sort of torture, since the machine does not free the labourer from work, but deprives the work of all interest. Every kind of capitalist production has this in common, that it is not the workman that employs the instruments of labour, but the instruments of labour that employ the workman. But it is only in the factory system that this inversion for the first time acquires technical and palpable reality. By means of its conversion into an automaton, the instrument of labour confronts the labourer, during the labour-process, in the shape of capital, of dead labour, that dominates, and pumps dry, living labour-power.

The technical subordination of the workman to the uniform motion of the instruments of labour, and the peculiar composition of the body of workpeople, consisting as it does of individuals of both sexes and of all ages, give rise to a barrack discipline, which is elabourated into a complete system in the factory, and which fully develops the before mentioned labour of overlooking, thereby dividing the workpeople into operatives and over lookers, into private soldiers and sergeants of an industrial army. The factory code in which capital formulates his autocracy over his workpeople, is but the capitalistic caricature of that social regulation of the labour-process. The place of the slave driver's lash is taken by the overlooker's book of penalties. Is Fourier wrong when he calls factories "tempered bagnios"?

The contest between the capitalist and the wage labourer dates back to the very origin of capital. It raged on throughout the whole manufacturing period. But only since the introduction of machinery has the workman fought against the instrument of labour itself, the material embodiment of capital. He revolts against this particular form of the means of production, as being the material basis of the capitalist mode of production.

In the 17th century nearly all Europe experienced revolts of the workpeople against the ribbon-loom. A wind-sawmill, erected near London by a Dutchman, succumbed to the excesses of the populace. No sooner had Everet in 1758 erected the first wool-shearing machine that was driven by water-power, than it was set on fire by 100,000 people who had been thrown out of work. The enormous destruction of machinery that occurred in the English manufacturing districts, known as the Luddite movement, gave governments a pretext for the most reactionary and forcible measures. It took both time and experience before the workpeople learnt to distinguish between machinery and its employment by capital, and to direct their attacks, not against the material instruments of production, but against the mode in which they are used.

The instrument of labour, when it takes the form of a machine, immediately becomes a competitor of the workman himself. When machinery seizes on an industry by degrees, it produces chronic misery among the operatives who compete with it. Where the transition is rapid, the effect is acute and felt by great masses. The instrument of labour strikes down the labourer.

In Modern Industry the continual improvement of machinery and the development of the automatic system have an analogous effect. Who, in 1860, the Zenith year of the English cotton industry, would have dreamt of the galloping improvements in machinery, and the corresponding displacement of working people, called into being during the following 3 years, under the stimulus of the American Civil War? Between 1861 and 1868, the number of spindles increased by 1,612,541, while the number of operatives decreased by 50,505.

Machinery is the most powerful weapon for repressing strikes, those periodical revolts of the working class against the autocracy of capital. The steam-engine was from the very first an antagonist of human power, an antagonist that enabled the capitalist to tread under foot the growing claims of the workmen, who threatened the newly born factory system with a crisis. It would be possible to write quite a history of the inventions, made since 1830, for the sole purpose of supplying capital with weapons against the revolts of the working class.

The contradictions and antagonisms inseparable from the capitalist employment of machinery, do not exist, since they do not arise out of machinery, as such, but out of its capitalist employment! It is an undoubted fact that machinery, as such, is not responsible for "setting free" the workman from the means of subsistence.

In proportion as machinery, with the aid of a relatively small number of workpeople, increases the mass of raw materials, intermediate products, instruments of labour, &c., the working-up of these raw materials and intermediate products becomes split up into numberless branches; social production increases in diversity. The factory system carries the social division of labour immeasurably further than does manufacture, for it increases the productiveness of the industries it seizes upon, in a far higher degree.

The immediate result of machinery is to augment surplus-value and the mass of products in which surplus value is embodied. And, as the substances consumed by the capitalists and their dependants become more plentiful, so too do these orders of society. Their growing wealth, and the relatively diminished number of workmen required to produce the necessaries of life beget, simultaneously with the rise of new and luxurious wants, the means of satisfying those wants. A larger portion of the produce of society is changed into surplus produce, and a larger part of the surplus produce is supplied for consumption in a multiplicity of refined shapes. In other words, the production of luxuries increases. Lastly, the extraordinary productiveness of modern industry, accompanied as it is by both a more extensive and a more intense exploitation of labour power in all other spheres of production, allows of the unproductive employment of a larger and larger part of the working class, and the consequent reproduction, on a constantly extending scale, of the ancient domestic slaves under the name of a servant class.

The increase of the means of production and subsistence, accompanied by a relative diminution in the number of labourers, causes an increased demand for labour in making canals, docks, tunnels, bridges, and so on, works that can only bear fruit in the far future. Entirely new branches of production, creating new fields of labour, are also formed, as the direct result either of machinery or of the general industrial changes brought about by it.

So long as, in a given branch of industry, the factory system extends itself at the expense of the old handicrafts or of manufacture, the result is as sure as is the result of an encounter between any army furnished with breach-loaders, and one armed with bows and arrows.

This first period, during which machinery conquers its field of action, is of decisive importance owing to the extraordinary profits that it helps to produce. So soon, however, as the factory system has gained a certain breadth of footing and a definite degree of maturity, and, especially, so soon as its technical basis, machinery, is itself produced by machinery; so soon as coal mining and iron mining, the metal industries, and the means of transport have been revolutionised; so soon, in short, as the general conditions requisite for production by the modern industrial system have been established, this mode of production acquires an elasticity, a capacity for sudden extension by leaps and bounds that finds no hindrance except in the supply of raw material and in the disposal of the produce. On the one hand, the effect of machinery is to increase the supply of raw material. On the other hand, the cheapness of the articles produced by machinery and the improved means of transport and communication furnish the weapons for conquering foreign markets.

By constantly making a part of the hands "supernumerary," modern industry, in all countries where it has taken root, gives a spur to emigration and to the colonisation of foreign lands, which are thereby converted into settlements for growing the raw material of the mother country. A new and international division of labour, a division suited to the requirements of the chief centres of modern industry springs up, and converts one part of the globe into a chiefly agricultural field of production, for supplying the other part which remains a chiefly industrial field. This evolution hangs together with radical changes in agriculture which we need not here further inquire into.

The enormous power, inherent in the factory system, of expanding by jumps, and the dependence of that system on the markets of the world, necessarily beget feverish production, followed by over-filling of the markets, whereupon contraction of the markets brings on crippling of production. The life of modern industry becomes a series of periods of moderate activity, prosperity, over-production, crisis and stagnation. The uncertainty and instability to which machinery subjects the employment, and consequently the conditions of existence, of the operatives become normal, owing to these periodic changes of the industrial cycle. Except in the periods of prosperity, there rages between the capitalists the most furious combat for the share of each in the markets.

The qualitative change in mechanical industry continually discharges hands from the factory, or shuts its doors against the fresh stream of recruits, while the purely quantitative extension of the factories absorbs not only the men thrown out of work, but also fresh contingents. The workpeople are thus continually both repelled and attracted, hustled from pillar to post.

Production in all the other branches of industry not only extends, but alters its character. This is the case not only with all production on a large scale, whether employing machinery or not, but also with the so-called domestic industry, whether carried on in the houses of the workpeople or in small workshops. This modern so-called domestic industry has nothing, except the name, in common with the old-fashioned domestic industry, the existence of which presupposes independent urban handicrafts, independent peasant farming, and above all, a dwelling-house for the labourer and his family. That old fashioned industry has now been converted into an outside department of the factory, the manufactory, or the warehouse. Besides the factory operatives, the manufacturing workmen and the handicraftsmen, whom it concentrates in large masses at one spot, and directly commands, capital also sets in motion, by means of invisible threads, another army; that of the workers in the domestic industries, who dwell in the large towns and are also scattered over the face of the country.

Economy in the means of production, first systematically carried out in the factory system, and there, from the very beginning, coincident with the most reckless squandering of labour-power, and robbery of the conditions normally requisite for labour-this economy now shows its antagonistic and murderous side more and more in a given branch of industry, the less the social productive power of labour and the technical basis for combination of processes are developed in that branch.

So long as Factory legislation is confined to regulating the labour in factories, manufactories, &c., it is regarded as a mere interference with the exploiting rights of capital But when it comes to regulating the so-called "home-labour," it is immediately viewed as a direct attack on the patria potestas, on parental authority. The tender-hearted English Parliament long affected to shrink from taking this step. The force of facts, however, compelled it at last to acknowledge that modern industry, in overturning the economical foundation on which was based the traditional family, and the family labour corresponding to it, had also unloosened all traditional family ties. The rights of the children had to be proclaimed. The necessity for a generalisation of the Factory Acts, for transforming them from an exceptional law relating to mechanical spinning and weaving- into a law affecting social production as a whole, arose from the mode in which Modern Industry was historically developed. There are two circumstances that finally turn the scale: first, the experience that capital, so soon as it finds itself subject to legal control at one point, compensates itself all the more recklessly at other points; secondly, the cry of the capitalists for equality in the conditions of competition, i.e., for equal restraint on all exploitation of labour.

If the general extension of factory legislation to all trades for the purpose of protecting the working class in both mind and body has become inevitable, on the other hand that extension hastens on the general conversion of numerous isolated small industries into a few combined industries carried on upon a large scale; it therefore accelerates the concentration of capital and the exclusive predominance of the factory system. It destroys both the ancient and the transitional forms, behind which the dominion of capital is still in part concealed, and replaces them by the direct and open sway of capital; but thereby it also generalises the direct opposition to this sway. While in each individual workshop it enforces uniformity, regularity, order, and economy, it increases by the immense spur which the limitation and regulation of the working day give to technical improvement, the anarchy and the catastrophes of capitalist production as a whole, the intensity of labour, and the competition of machinery with the labourer. By the destruction of petty and domestic industries it destroys the last resort of the "redundant population," and with it the sole remaining safety-valve of the whole social mechanism. By maturing the material conditions, and the combination on a social scale of the processes of production, it matures the contradictions and antagonisms of the capitalist form of production, and thereby provides, along with the elements for the formation of a new society, the forces for exploding the old one. In the sphere of agriculture, modern industry has a more revolutionary effect than elsewhere, for this reason, that it annihilates the peasant, that bulwark of the old society, and replaces him by the wage labourer. Thus the desire for social changes, and the class antagonisms are brought to the same level in the country as in the towns. The irrational, old-fashioned methods of agriculture are replaced by scientific ones. In agriculture as in manufacture, the transformation of production under the sway of capital means, at the same time, the martyrdom of the producer; the instrument of labour becomes the means of enslaving, exploiting, and impoverishing the labourer; the social combination and organisation of labour-processes is turned into an organised mode of crushing out the workman's individual vitality, freedom and independence. The dispersion of the rural labourers over larger areas breaks their power of resistance while concentration increases that of the town operatives. In modern agriculture, as in the urban industries, the increased productiveness and quantity of the labour set in motion are bought at the cost of laying waste and consuming by disease labour power itself. Moreover, all progress in capitalistic agriculture is a progress in the art, not only of robbing the labourer, but of robbing the soil; all progress in increasing the fertility of the soil for a given time, is a progress towards ruining the lasting sources of that fertility. The more a country starts its development on the foundation of modern industry, like the United States, for example, the more rapid is this process of destruction. Capitalistic production, therefore, develops technology and the combining together of various processes into a social whole, only by sapping the original sources of all wealth — the soil and the labourer.

Part 5
The Production of Absolute and of Relative Surplus-Value
Chapter Sixteen: Absolute and Relative Surplus-Value

As the co-operative character of the labour-process becomes more and more marked, so, as a necessary consequence, does our notion of productive labour, and of its agent the productive labourer, become extended. In order to labour productively, it is no longer necessary for you to do manual work yourself; enough, if you are an organ of the collective labourer, and perform one of its subordinate functions. In another sense, however, our notion of productive labour becomes narrowed. That labourer alone is productive, who produces surplus-value for the capitalist, and thus works for the self-expansion of capital. Hence the notion of a productive labourer implies not merely a relation between work and useful effect, between labourer and product of labour, but also a specific, social relation of production, a relation that has sprung up historically and stamps the labourer as the direct means of creating surplus-value. In the course of this development, the formal subjection is replaced by the real subjection of labour to capital.

From one standpoint, any distinction between absolute and relative surplus-value appears illusory. Relative surplus-value is absolute, since it compels the absolute prolongation of the working day beyond the labour time necessary to the existence of the labourer himself. Absolute surplus-value is relative, since it makes necessary such a development of the productiveness of labour, as will allow of the necessary labour-time being confined to a portion of the working day. But if we keep in mind the behaviour of surplus-value, this appearance of identity vanishes. Once the capitalist mode of production is established and becomes general, the difference between absolute and relative surplus-value makes itself felt.

Assuming that labour-power is paid for at its value, we are confronted by this alternative: given the productiveness of labour and its normal intensity, the rate of surplus-value can be raised only by the actual prolongation of the working day; on the other hand, given the length of the working day, that rise can be effected only by a change in the relative magnitudes of the components of the working day, viz., necessary labour and surplus-labour; a change, which, if the wages are not to fall below the value of labour-power, presupposes a change either in the productiveness or in the intensity of the labour.

Thus, not only does the historically developed social productiveness of labour, but also its natural productiveness, appear to be productiveness of the capital with which that labour is incorporated. Favourable natural conditions alone gave us only the possibility, never the reality, of surplus-labour, nor, consequently, of surplus-value and a surplus-product. The result of difference in the natural conditions of labour is this, that the same quantity of labour satisfies, in different countries, a different mass of requirements, consequently, that under circumstances in other respects analogous, the necessary labour-time is different. These conditions affect surplus-labour only as natural limits, i.e., by fixing the points at which labour for others can begin. In proportion as industry advances, these natural limits recede.

Chapter Seventeen: Changes of Magnitude in the Price of Labour-Power and in Surplus-Value

On the assumptions (1) that commodities are sold at their value; and (2) that the price of labour-power rises occasionally above its value, but never sinks below it, we have seen that the relative magnitudes of surplus-value and of price of labour-power are determined by three circumstances: (1) the length of the working day, or the extensive magnitude of labour; (2) the normal intensity of labour, its intensive magnitude, whereby a given quantity of labour is expended in a given time; and (3) the productiveness of labour. Very different combinations are clearly possible.

The chief combinations are:

I. Length of the working day and intensity of labour constant. Productiveness of labour variable.

II. Working day constant. Productiveness of labour constant. Intensity of labour variable.

III. Productiveness and intensity of labour constant. Length of the working day variable.

IV. Simultaneous variations in the duration, productiveness, and intensity of labour.

Chapter Eighteen: Various Formulae for the Rate of Surplus-Value

The rate of surplus-value is represented by the following formulae:

I. Surplus-value/Variable Capital (s/v) = Surplus-value/Value of labour-power = Surplus-labour/Necessary labour

The first two of these formulae represent, as a ratio of values, that which, in the third, is represented as a ratio of the times during which those values are produced. These formulae, supplementary the one to the other, are rigorously definite and correct. In classical political economy we meet with the following derivative formulae:

II. Surplus-labour/Working day = Surplus-value/Value of the Product = Surplus-product/Total Product

One and the same ratio is here expressed as a ratio of labour-times, of the values in which those labour-times are embodied, and of the products in which those values exist.

In all of these formulae (II), the actual degree of exploitation of labour, or the rate of surplus-value, is falsely expressed. Let the working day be 12 hours. Then, making the same assumptions of former instances, the real degree of exploitation of labour will be represented in the following proportions: 6 hours surplus labour/6 hours necessary labour = Surplus-value of 3sh/Variable Capital of 3 sh = 100%

From formulae II we get very differently, 6 hours surplus-labour/Working day of 12 hours = Surplus-value of 3 sh/Value created of 6 sh = 50%

These derivative formulae express, in reality, only the proportion in which the working day, or the value produced by it, is divided between capitalist and labourer. If they are to be treated as direct expressions of the degree of self-expansion of capital, the following erroneous law would hold good: Surplus-labour or surplus-value can never reach 100%. Since the surplus labour is only an aliquot part of the working day, or since surplus-value is only an aliquot part of the value created, the surplus-labour must necessarily be always less than the working day, or the surplus-value always less than the total value created. The ratio Surplus labour/Working day or Surplus Value/Value created can therefore never reach the limit of 100/100 still less rise to 100 + x/100. But not so the rate of surplus-value, the real degree of exploitation of labour. There is a third formula; it is:

III. Surplus-value / Value of labour power = Surplus-labour / Necessary labour = Unpaid labour / Paid labour.

It is no longer possible to be misled, by the formula Unpaid labour / Paid labour, into concluding, that the capitalist pays for labour and not for labour-power. The capitalist pays the value of the labour-power, and receives in exchange the disposal of the living labour-power itself. Thus the capitalist receives in return for the price a product of the same price. During the period of surplus labour, the usufruct of the labour-power creates a value for the capitalist. This expenditure of labour-power comes to him gratis. In this sense it is that surplus labour can be called unpaid labour.

Capital, therefore, is not only, as Adam Smith says, the command over labour. It is essentially the command over unpaid labour. All surplus-value, whatever particular form (profit, interest, or rent), it may subsequently crystallise into, is in substance the materialisation of unpaid labour. The secret of the self-expansion of capital resolves itself into having the disposal of a definite quantity of other people's unpaid labour.

Part 6
Wages
Chapter Nineteen: The Transformation of the Value (and respectively the Price) of Labour-Power into Wages

On the surface of bourgeois society the wage of the labourer appears as the price of labour, a certain quantity of money that is paid for a certain quantity of labour. That which comes directly face to face with the possessor of money on the market, is in fact not labour, but the labourer. What the latter sells is his labour power. As soon as his labour actually begins, it has already ceased to belong to him; it can therefore no longer be sold by him. Labour is the substance, and the immanent measure of value, but has itself no value.

The wage-form extinguishes every trace of the division of the working day into necessary labour and surplus-labour, into paid and unpaid labour. All labour appears as paid labour.

In slave-labour, even that part of the working day in which the slave is only replacing the value of his own means of existence, in which, therefore, in fact, he works for himself alone, appears as labour for his master. All the slave's labour appears as unpaid labour. In wage-labour, on the contrary, even surplus-labour, or unpaid labour, appears as paid.

Let us put ourselves in the place of the labourer who receives for 12 hours' labour, say the value produced by 6 hours' labour, say 3s. For him, in fact, his 12 hours' labour is the means of buying the 3s. The value of his labour-power may vary, with the value of his usual means of subsistence, from 3 to 4 shillings, or from 3 to 2 shillings; or, if the value of his labour-power remains constant, its price may, in consequence of changing relations of demand and supply rise to 4s. or fall to 2s. He always gives 12 hours of labour. Every change in the amount of the equivalent that he receives appears to him necessarily as a change in the value or price of his 12 hours' work.

Let us consider, on the other hand, the capitalist. He wishes to receive as much labour as possible for as little money as possible. Practically, therefore, the only thing that interests him is the difference between the price of labour-power and the value which its function creates. But, then, he tries to buy all commodities as cheaply as possible, and always accounts for his profit by simple cheating, by buying under, and selling over the value. Hence, he never comes to see that, if such a thing as the value of labour really existed and he really paid this value, no capital would exist, his money would not be turned into capital.

Chapter Twenty: Time-Wages

The sale of labour-power takes place for a definite period of time. The converted form under which the daily, weekly, &c., value of labour-power presents itself, is hence that of time-wages, therefore day-wages, &c.

The sum of money which the labourer receives for his daily or weekly labour, forms the amount of his nominal wages, or of his wages estimated in value. But it is clear that according to the length of the working day, that, is, according to the amount of actual labour daily supplied, the same daily or weekly wage may represent very different prices of labour. We must, therefore, in considering time-wages, again distinguish between the sum total of the daily or weekly wages, &c., and the price of labour.

How then to find this price, i.e., the money-value of a given quantity of labour?

The average price of labour is found, when the average daily value of the labour-power is divided by the average number of hours in the working day. The price of the working hour thus found serves as the unit measure for the price of labour.

The daily and weekly wages, &c., may remain the same, although the price of labour falls constantly. On the contrary, the daily or weekly wages may rise, although the price of labour remains constant or even falls. As a general law it follows that, given the amount of daily, weekly labour, &c., the daily or weekly wages depend on the price of labour, which itself varies either with the value of labour-power, or with the difference between its price and its value. Given, on the other hand, the price of labour, the daily or weekly wages depend on the quantity of the daily or weekly labour.

If the hour's wage is fixed so that the capitalist does not bind himself to pay a day's or a week's wage, but only to pay wages for the hours during which he chooses to employ the labourer, he can employ him for a shorter time than that which is originally the basis of the calculation of the hour-wage, of the unit-measure of the price of labour.

He can now wring from the labourer a certain quantity of surplus-labour without allowing him the labour time necessary for his own subsistence. He can annihilate all regularity of employment, and according to his own convenience, caprice, and the interest of the moment, make the most enormous over-work alternate with relative or absolute cessation of work. He can, under the pretence of paying "the normal price of labour," abnormally lengthen the working day without any corresponding compensation to the labourer.

With an increasing daily or weekly wage the price of labour may remain nominally constant, and yet may fall below its normal level. This occurs every time that, the price of labour (reckoned per working hour) remaining constant, the working day is prolonged beyond its customary length. It is a fact generally known that, the longer the working days, in any branch of industry, the lower are the wages. The same circumstances which allow the capitalist in the long run to prolong the working day, also allow him first, and compel him finally, nominally to lower the price of labour until the total price of the increased number of hours is lowered, and, therefore, the daily or weekly wage.

This command over abnormal quantities of unpaid labour, i.e., quantities in excess of the average social amount, becomes a source of competition amongst the capitalists themselves. A part of the price of the commodity consists of the price of labour.

Chapter Twenty-One: Piece-Wages

Wages by the piece are nothing else than a converted form of wages by time. In time-wages the labour is measured by its immediate duration, in piece-wages by the quantity of products in which the labour has embodied itself during a given time. It is not, therefore, a question of measuring the value of the piece by the working time incorporated in it, but on the contrary of measuring the working time the labourer has expended, by the number of pieces he has produced.

Piece-wages furnish to the capitalist an exact measure for the intensity of labour. Only the working time which is embodied in a quantum of commodities determined beforehand and experimentally fixed counts as socially necessary working time, and is paid as such. The quality of the labour is here controlled by the work itself, which must be of average perfection if the piece price is to be paid in full. Piece-wages become, from this point of view, the most fruitful source of reductions of wages and capitalistic cheating.

Since the quality and intensity of the work are here controlled by the form of wage itself, superintendence of labour becomes in great part superfluous. Piece wages therefore lay the foundation of the modern "domestic labour", as well as of a hierarchically organised system of exploitation and oppression. The latter has two fundamental forms: the interposition of parasites between the capitalist and the wage-labourer, and the "sub-letting of labour."

The exploitation of the labourer by capital is here effected through the exploitation of the labourer by the labourer.

In time-wages, with few exceptions, the same wage holds for the same kind of work, whilst in piece-wages, though the price of the working time is measured by a certain quantity of product, the day's or week's wage will vary with the individual differences of the labourers, of whom one supplies in a given time the minimum of product only, another the average, a third more than the average. With regard to actual receipts there is, therefore, great variety according to the different skill, strength, energy, staying-power, etc., of the individual labourers.

Of course this does not alter the general relations between capital and wage-labour. First, the individual differences balance one another in the workshop as a whole, which thus supplies in a given working-time the average product, and the total wages paid will be the average wages of that particular branch of industry. Second, the proportion between wages and surplus value remains unaltered, since the mass of surplus-labour supplied by each particular labourer corresponds with the wage received by him. But the wider scope that piece-wage gives to individuality tends to develop on the one hand that individuality, and with it the sense of liberty, independence, and self-control of the labourers, on the other, their competition one with another. Piece-work has, therefore, a tendency, while raising individual wages above the average, to lower this average itself.

Piece-wage is the form of wages most in harmony with the capitalist mode of production. It only conquers a larger field for action during the period of Manufacture, properly so-called. In the stormy youth of Modern Industry, it served as a lever for the lengthening of the working day, and the lowering of wages. In the workshops under the Factory Acts, piece-wage becomes the general rule, because capital can there only increase the efficacy of the working day by intensifying labour.

Chapter Twenty-Two: National Differences of Wages

In every country there is a certain average intensity of labour, below which the labour for the production of a commodity requires more than the socially necessary time, and therefore does not reckon as labour of normal quality. Only a degree of intensity above the national average affects, in a given country, the measure of value of the mere duration of the working time. This is not the case on the universal market, whose integral parts are the individual countries.

The average intensity of labour changes from country to country; here it is greater, there less. These national averages form a scale, whose unit of measure is the average unit of universal labour. The more intense national labour, therefore, as compared with the less intense, produces in the same time more value, which expresses itself in more money.

The relative value of money will be less in the nation with more developed capitalist mode of production than in the nation with less developed. It follows, then, that the nominal wages, the equivalent of labour-power expressed in money, will also be higher in the first nation than in the second, which does not at all prove that this holds also for the real wages, i.e., for the means of subsistence placed at the disposal of the labourer.

Part 7
The Accumulation of Capital

The conversion of a sum of money into means of production and labour-power is the first step taken by the quantum of value that is going to function as capital. This conversion takes place in the market, within the sphere of circulation. The second step, the process of production, is complete so soon as the means of production have been converted into commodities whose value exceeds that of their component parts, and, therefore, contains the capital originally advanced, plus a surplus-value. These commodities must then be thrown into circulation. They must be sold, their value realised in money, this money afresh converted into capital, and so over and over again. This movement forms the circulation of capital.

Chapter Twenty-Three: Simple Reproduction

A society can no more cease to produce than it can cease to consume. Therefore, every social process of production is, at the same time, a process of reproduction.

The conditions of production are also those of reproduction. If production be capitalistic in form, so, too, will be reproduction. Just as in the former the labour-process figures but as a means towards the self-expansion of capital, so in the latter it figures but as a means of reproducing as capital the value advanced. It is only because his money constantly functions as capital that the economical guise of a capitalist attaches to a man.

Simple reproduction is a mere repetition of the process of production on the old scale. As a periodic increment of the capital advanced, or periodic fruit of capital in process, surplus-value acquires the form of a revenue flowing out of capital.

The value of the capital advanced divided by the surplus-value annually consumed, gives the number of years, or reproduction periods, at the expiration of which the capital originally advanced has been consumed by the capitalist and has disappeared. After the lapse of a certain number of years the capital value he then possesses is equal to the sum total of the surplus-value appropriated by him during those years, and the total value he has consumed is equal to that of his original capital.

The mere continuity of the process of production, in other words simple reproduction, sooner or later, and of necessity, converts every capital into accumulated capital, or capitalised surplus-value. If that capital was originally acquired by the personal labour of its employer, it sooner or later becomes value appropriated without an equivalent, the unpaid labour of others materialised either in money or in some other object.

That which at first was but a starting point, becomes, by the mere continuity of the process, by simple reproduction, the peculiar result, constantly renewed and perpetuated, of capitalist production. On the one hand, the process of production incessantly converts material wealth into capital, into means of creating more wealth and means of enjoyment for the capitalist. On the other hand the labourer, on quitting the process, is what he was on entering it, a source of wealth, but devoid of all means of making that wealth his own. The labourer constantly produces material, objective wealth, but in the form of capital, of an alien power that dominates and exploits him; and the capitalist as constantly produces labour-power, but in the form of a subjective source of wealth, separated from the objects in and by which it can alone be realised; in short he produces the labourer, but as a wage-labourer.

The labourer consumes in a twofold way. While producing he consumes by his labour the means of production, and converts them into products with a higher value than that of the capital advanced. This is his productive consumption. On the other hand, the labourer turns the money paid to him for his labour power, into means of subsistence: this is his individual consumption. Productive consumption and individual consumption are totally distinct. In the former, he acts as the motive power of capital, and belongs to the capitalist. In the latter, he belongs to himself, and performs his necessary vital functions outside the process of production. The result of the one is, that the capitalist lives; of the other, that the labourer lives.

By converting part of his capital into labour-power, the capitalist augments the value of his entire capital. He kills two birds with one stone. He profits, not only by what he receives from, but by what he gives to, the labourer. The capital is converted into necessaries, by the consumption of which the muscles, nerves, bones, and brains of existing labourers are reproduced, and new labourers are begotten.

The individual consumption of the working class is, therefore, the production and reproduction of that means of production so indispensable to the capitalist: the labourer himself. The maintenance and reproduction of the working class is, and must ever be, a necessary condition to the reproduction of capital. Hence the capitalist considers that part alone of the labourer's individual consumption to be productive, which is requisite for the perpetuation of the class; what the labourer consumes for his own pleasure beyond that part, is unproductive consumption. In reality, the individual consumption of the labourer is unproductive as regards himself, for it reproduces nothing but the needy individual; it is productive to the capitalist and the State, since it is the production of the power that creates their wealth.

From a social point of view, therefore, the working class, even when not directly engaged in the labour process, is just as much an appendage of capital as the ordinary instruments of labour. Even its individual consumption is, within certain limits, a mere factor in the process of production. The Roman slave was held by fetters: the wage-labourer is bound to his owner by invisible threads. The reproduction of the working class carries with it the accumulation of skill that is handed down from one generation to another.

Capitalist production reproduces the separation between labour-power and the means of labour. It thereby reproduces and perpetuates the condition for exploiting. It incessantly forces him to sell his labour-power in order to live, and enables the capitalist to purchase labour power in order that he may enrich himself. It is no longer a mere accident, that capitalist and labourer confront each other in the market as buyer and seller. It is the process itself that incessantly hurls back the labourer on to the market as a vendor of his labour-power, and that incessantly converts his own product into a means by which another man can purchase him. In reality, the labourer belongs to capital before he has sold himself to capital. His economical bondage is both brought about and concealed by the periodic sale of himself, by his change of masters, and by the oscillations in the market price of labour-power.

Capitalist production, therefore, under its aspect of a continuous connected process, of a process of reproduction, produces not only commodities, not only surplus-value, but it also produces and reproduces the capitalist relation.

Chapter Twenty-Four: Conversion of Surplus-Value into Capital

Employing surplus-value as capital, reconverting it into capital, is called accumulation of capital.

To accumulate, it is necessary to convert a portion of the surplus-product into capital. But we cannot, except by a miracle, convert into capital anything but such articles as can be employed in the labour-process (i.e., means of production), and means of subsistence. Consequently, a part of the annual surplus-labour must have been applied to the production of additional means of production and subsistence, over and above the quantity of these things required to replace the capital advanced. In one word, surplus-value is convertible into capital solely because the surplus-product, whose value it is, already comprises the material elements of new capital. In order to allow of these elements actually functioning, the capitalist class requires additional labour. If the exploitation of the labourers already employed should not increase, either extensively or intensively, then additional labour-power must be found. For this the mechanism of capitalist production provides beforehand, by converting the working class into a class dependent on wages, a class whose ordinary wages suffice, not only for its maintenance, but for its increase. It is only necessary for capital to incorporate this additional labour power, with the surplus means of production, and the conversion of surplus-value into capital is complete.

It is the old story: Abraham begat Isaac, Isaac begat Jacob, and so on. The original capital of £10,000 brings in a surplus-value of £2,000, which is capitalised. The new capital of £2000 brings in a surplus-value of £400, and this, too, is capitalised, converted into a second additional capital, and, in its turn, produces a further surplus-value of £80. And so the ball rolls on.

At first the rights of property seemed to us to be based on a man's own labour. At least, some such assumption was necessary since only commodity owners with equal rights confronted each other, and the sole means by which a man could become possessed of the commodities of others, was by alienating his own commodities; and these could be replaced by labour alone. Now, however, property turns out to be the right, on the part of the capitalist, to appropriate the unpaid labour of others or its product and to be the impossibility, on the part of the labourer, of appropriating his own product. The separation of property from labour has become the necessary consequence of a law that apparently originated in their identity.

We have seen that even in the case of simple reproduction, all capital, whatever its original source, becomes converted into accumulated capital, capitalised surplus-value. But in the flood of production all the capital originally advanced becomes a vanishing quantity (magnitudo evanescens, in the mathematical sense), compared with the directly accumulated capital, i.e., with the surplus-value or surplus product that is reconverted into capital, whether it function in the hands of its accumulator, or in those of others. One portion is consumed by the capitalist as revenue, the other is employed as capital, is accumulated. Given the mass of surplus-value, then, the larger the one of these parts, the smaller is the other. The ratio of these parts determines the magnitude of the accumulation. But it is by the owner of the surplus-value, by the capitalist alone, that the division is made. It is his deliberate act. Except as personified capital, the capitalist has no historical value, and no right to existence.

Only as personified capital is the capitalist respectable. As such, he shares with the miser the passion for wealth as wealth. Fanatically bent on making value expand itself, he ruthlessly forces the human race to produce for production's sake; he thus forces the development of the productive powers of society, and creates those material conditions, which alone can form the real basis of a higher form of society. To accumulate is to conquer the world of social wealth, to increase the mass of human beings exploited by him, and thus to extend both the direct and the indirect sway of the capitalist.

At the historical dawn of capitalist production — and every capitalist upstart has personally to go through this historical stage — avarice, and desire to get rich, are the ruling passions. But the progress not only creates a world of delights; it lays open, in speculation and the credit system, a thousand sources of sudden enrichment. When a certain stage of development has been reached, a conventional degree of prodigality, which is also an exhibition of wealth, and consequently a source of credit, becomes a business necessity to the "unfortunate" capitalist. Luxury enters into capital's expenses of representation. Although, therefore, the prodigality of the capitalist never possesses the bona-fide character of the open-handed feudal lord's prodigality, but, on the contrary, has always lurking behind it the most sordid avarice and the most anxious calculation, yet his expenditure grows with his accumulation. Circumstances that, independently of the division of surplus-value into capital and revenue, determine the amount of accumulation are: degree of exploitation of labour-power; productivity of labour; growing difference in amount between capital employed and capital consumed; magnitude of capital advanced. By incorporating with itself the two primary creators of wealth, labour-power and the land, capital acquires a power of expansion that permits it to augment the elements of its accumulation beyond the limits apparently fixed by its own magnitude, or by the value and the mass of the means of production, already produced, in which it has its being.

An important factor in the accumulation of capital is the degree of productivity of social labour. The development of the productive power of labour reacts also on the original capital already engaged in the process of production. The old capital is reproduced in a more productive form. Every introduction of improved methods works almost simultaneously on the new capital and on that already in action. Every advance in Chemistry not only multiplies the number of useful materials and the useful applications of those already known, thus extending with the growth of capital its sphere of investment. It teaches at the same time how to throw the excrements of the processes of production and consumption back again into the circle of the process of reproduction, and thus, without any previous outlay of capital, creates new matter for capital. Like the increased exploitation of natural wealth by the mere increase in the tension of labour-power, science and technology give capital a power of expansion independent of the given magnitude of the capital actually functioning. They react at the same time on that part of the original capital which has entered upon its stage of renewal. This, in passing into its new shape, incorporates gratis the social advance made while its old shape was being used up. Hence, with the increase in efficacy, extent and value of its means of production, labour keeps up and eternises an always increasing capital-value in a form ever new. This natural power of labour takes the appearance of an intrinsic property of capital.

Chapter Twenty-Five: The General Law of Capitalist Accumulation

The composition of capital is to be understood in a twofold sense. On the side of value, it is determined by the proportion in which it is divided into constant and variable capital. On the side of material, as it functions in the process of production, all capital is divided into means of production and living labour-power. I call the former the value-composition, the latter the technical composition of capital. Between the two there is a strict correlation. I call the value-composition of capital, in so far as it is determined by its technical composition and mirrors the changes of the latter, the organic composition of capital.

The many individual capitals invested in a particular branch of production have, one with another, more or less different compositions. The average of their individual compositions gives the composition of the total capital in this branch of production. Lastly, the average of these averages, in all branches of production, gives the composition of the total social capital of a country, and with this alone are we concerned in the following investigation. Growth of capital involves growth of its variable constituent. A part of the surplus-value turned into additional capital must always be retransformed into variable capital, or additional labour-fund. If we suppose that a definite mass of means of production constantly needs the same mass of labour-power then the demand for labour and the subsistence-fund of the labourers clearly increase in the same proportion as the capital, and the more rapidly, the more rapidly the capital increases. The requirements of accumulating capital may exceed the increase of labour-power or of the number of labourers; the demand for labourers may exceed the supply and, therefore, wages may rise.

As simple reproduction constantly reproduces the capital-relation itself, i.e., the relation of capitalists on the one hand, and wage-workers on the other, so reproduction on a progressive scale, i.e., accumulation, reproduces the capital-relation on a progressive scale, more capitalists or larger capitalists at this pole, more wage workers at that. The reproduction of a mass of labour power, which must incessantly re-incorporate itself with capital for that capital's self-expansion; which cannot get free from capital, and whose enslavement to capital is only concealed by the variety of individual capitalists to whom it sells itself, this reproduction of labour-power forms, in fact, an essential of the reproduction of capital itself. Accumulation of capital is, therefore, increase of the proletariat.

Under the conditions of accumulation, which conditions are those most favourable to the labourers, their relation of dependence upon capital takes on a form endurable. A larger part of their own surplus-product, always increasing and continually transformed into additional capital, comes back to them in the shape of means of payment, so that they can extend the circle of their enjoyments; can make some additions to their consumption-fund of clothes, furniture, &c., and can lay by small reserve-funds of money. But just as little as better clothing, food, and treatment, and a larger peculium, do away with the exploitation of the slave, so little do they set aside that of the wage-worker. A rise in the price of labour, as a consequence of accumulation of capital, only means, in fact, that the length and weight of the golden chain the wage-worker has already forged for himself, allow of a relaxation of the tension of it.

With the use of machinery, a greater mass of raw material and auxiliary substances enter into the labour process. That is the consequence of the increasing productivity of labour. On the other hand, the mass of machinery, beasts of burden, mineral manures, drainpipes, &c., is a condition of the increasing productivity of labour. So also is it with the means of production concentrated in buildings, furnaces, means of transport, &c. But whether condition or consequence, the growing extent of the means of production, as compared with the labour-power incorporated with them, is an expression of the growing productiveness of labour. The increase of the latter appears in the diminution of the mass of labour in proportion to the mass of mean; of production moved by it, or in the diminution of the subjective factor of the labour process as compared with the objective factor.

This change in the technical composition of capital this growth in the mass of means of production, as compared with the mass of the labour-power that vivifies them, is reflected again in its value-composition, by the increase of the constant constituent of capital at the expense of its variable constituent. This law of the progressive increase in constant capital, in proportion to the variable, is confirmed at every step by the comparative analysis of the prices of commodities, whether we compare different economic epochs or different nation in the same epoch. The relative magnitude of the element of price, which represents the value of the mean of production only, or the constant part of capital consumed, is in direct, the relative magnitude of the other element of price that pays labour (the variable part of capital) is in inverse proportion to the advance of accumulation. This diminution in the variable part of capital as compared with the constant, or the altered value composition of the capital, however, only shows approximately the change in the composition of its material constituents. With the increasing productivity of labour, not only does the mass of the means of production consumed by it increase, but their value compared with their mass diminishes. Their value therefore rises absolutely, but not in proportion to their mass. The increase of the difference between constant and variable capital is, therefore, much less than that of the difference between the mass of the means of production into which the constant, and the mass of the labour-power into which the variable, capital is converted. The former difference increases with the latter, but in a smaller degree. But, if the progress of accumulation lessens the relative magnitude of the variable part of capital, it by no means, in doing this, excludes the possibility of a rise in its absolute magnitude.

Every individual capital is a larger or smaller concentration of means of production, with a corresponding command over a larger or smaller labour-army. Every accumulation becomes the means of new accumulation. Accumulation increases the concentration of that wealth in the hands of individual capitalists, and thereby widens the basis of production on a large scale and of the specific methods of capitalist production. The growth of social capital is effected by the growth of many individual capitals. All other circumstances remaining the same, individual capitals, and with them the concentration of the means of production, increases in such proportion as they form aliquot parts of the total social capital.

Accumulation, therefore, presents itself on the one hand as increasing concentration of the means of production, and of the command over labour; on the other, as repulsion of many individual capitals one from another. This splitting-up of the total social capital into many individual capitals or the repulsion of its fractions one from another, is counteracted by their attraction. This last does not mean simple concentration, which is identical with accumulation. It is concentration of capitals already formed, destruction of their individual independence, expropriation of capitalist by capitalist, transformation of many small into few large capitals. This process differs from the former in this, that it only presupposes a change in the distribution of capital already to hand, and functioning; its field of action is therefore not limited by the absolute growth of social wealth, by the absolute limits of accumulation. Capital grows in one place to a huge mass in a single hand, because it has in another place been lost by many. This is centralisation proper, as distinct from accumulation and concentration. Centralisation supplements the work of accumulation, by enabling the industrial capitalists to expand the scale of their operations. Whether centralisation is accomplished by the violent means of annexation, or whether it proceeds by the smoother road of forming stock companies, the economic result remains the same: progressive transformation of isolated processes of production carried on in accustomed ways into socially combined and scientifically managed processes of production.

The masses of capital amalgamated over night by centralisation reproduce and augment themselves like the others, only faster, and thus become new and powerful levers of social accumulation. The additional capitals serve mainly as vehicles for the exploitation of new inventions and discoveries, or of industrial improvements in general. However, the old capital likewise arrives in due time at the moment when it must renew its head and limbs, when it casts off its old skin and is likewise born again in its perfected industrial form, in which a smaller quantity of labour suffices to set in motion a larger quantity of machinery and raw materials. The absolute decrease of the demand for labour necessarily following therefrom will naturally be so much greater, the more these capitals going through the process of rejuvenation have become accumulated in masses by means of the movement of centralisation.

The labouring population produces, along with the accumulation of capital, the means by which itself is made relatively superfluous; and it does this to an always increasing extent. This is a law of population peculiar to the capitalist mode of production.

But if a surplus labouring population is a necessary product of accumulation or of the development of wealth on a capitalist basis, this surplus population becomes, conversely, the lever of capitalistic accumulation, nay, a condition of existence of the capitalist mode of production. It forms a disposable industrial reserve army, that belongs to capital quite as absolutely as if the latter had bred it at its own cost. Independently of the limits of the actual increase of population, it creates for the changing needs of the self-expansion of capital, a mass of human material always ready for exploitation.

The course characteristic of modern industry, viz., a decennial cycle (interrupted by smaller oscillations), of periods of average activity, production at high pressure, crisis and stagnation, depends on the constant formation, the greater or less absorption, and the reformation of the industrial reserve army of surplus population. In their turn, the varying phases of the industrial cycle recruit the surplus population, and become one of the most energetic agents of its reproduction. The whole form of the movement of modern industry depends upon the constant transformation of a part of the labouring population into unemployed or half-employed hands.

The setting free of labourers goes on yet more rapidly than the technical revolution of the process of production that accompanies, and is accelerated by, the advances of accumulation; and more rapidly than the corresponding diminution of the variable part of capital as compared with the constant. If the means of production, as they increase in extent and effective power, become to a less extent means of employment of labourers, this state of things is again modified by the fact that in proportion as the productiveness of labour increases, capital increases its supply of labour more quickly than its demand for labourers. The over-work of the employed part of the working class swells the ranks of the reserve, whilst conversely the greater pressure that the latter by its competition exerts on the former, forces these to submit to over-work and to subjugation under the dictates of capital. The condemnation of one part of the working class to enforced idleness by the over-work of the other part, and the converse, becomes a means of enriching the individual capitalists, and accelerates at the same time the production of the industrial reserve army on a scale corresponding with the advance of social accumulation.

Taking them as a whole, the general movements of wages are exclusively regulated by the expansion and contraction of the industrial reserve army, and these again correspond to the periodic changes of the industrial cycle. They are, therefore, not determined by the variations of the absolute number of the working population, but by the varying proportions in which the working class is divided into active and reserve army, by the increase and diminution in the relative amount of the surplus-population, by the extent to which it is now absorbed, now set free.

The industrial reserve army, during the periods of stagnation and average prosperity, weighs down the active labour-army; during the periods of over-production and paroxysm, it holds its pretensions in check. Relative surplus-population is therefore the pivot upon which the law of demand and supply of labour works. It confines the field of action of this law within the limits absolutely convenient to the activity of exploitation and to the domination of capital, and completes the despotism of capital.

The relative surplus population exists in every possible form. Every labourer belongs to it during the time when he is only partially employed or wholly unemployed. Not taking into account the great periodically recurring forms that the changing phases of the industrial cycle impress on it, now an acute form during the crisis, then again a chronic form during dull times — it has always three forms, the floating, the latent, the stagnant.

The consumption of labour-power by capital is, besides, so rapid that the labourer half-way through his life, has already more or less completely lived himself out. It is precisely among the workpeople of modern industry that we meet with the shortest duration of life. Hence, rapid renewal of the generations of labourers.

Not only the number of births and deaths, but the absolute size of the families stand in inverse proportion to the height of wages, and therefore to the amount of means of subsistence of which the different categories of labourers dispose. This law of capitalistic society would sound absurd to savages. It calls to mind the boundless reproduction of animals individually weak and constantly hunted down. As soon as capitalist production takes possession of agriculture, and in proportion to the extent to which it does so, the demand for an agricultural labouring population falls absolutely, while the accumulation of the capital employed in agriculture advances, without this repulsion being, as in non-agricultural industries, compensated by a greater attraction. Part of the agricultural population is therefore constantly on the point of passing over into an urban or manufacturing proletariat This source of relative surplus-population is constantly flowing. But the constant flow towards the towns presupposes, in the country itself, a constant latent surplus population. The agricultural labourer is therefore reduced to the minimum of wages, and always stands with one foot already in the swamp of pauperism.

The lowest sediment of the relative surplus-population finally dwells in the sphere of pauperism. Exclusive of vagabonds, criminals, prostitutes, in a word, the "dangerous" classes, this layer of society consists of three categories. First, those able to work. Second, orphans and pauper children. Third, the demoralised and ragged, those unable to work, the mutilated, the sickly, the widows, &c. Pauperism is the hospital of the active labour-army and the dead weight of the industrial reserve-army.

The greater the social wealth, the functioning capital, the extent and energy of its growth, and, therefore, also the absolute mass of the proletariat and the productiveness of its labour, the greater is the industrial reserve-army. The same causes which develop the expansive power of capital, develops also the labour power at its disposal. The relative mass of the industrial reserve-army increases therefore with the potential energy of wealth. But the greater this reserve-army in proportion to the active labour-army, the greater is the mass of a consolidated surplus-population, whose misery is in inverse ratio to its torment of labour. The more extensive, finally, the lazarus-layers of the working class, and the industrial reserve-army, the greater is official pauperism. This is the absolute general law of capitalist accumulation.

It follows therefore that in proportion as capital accumulates, the lot of the labourer, be his payment high or low, must grow worse. The law, finally, that always equilibrates the relative surplus-population, or industrial reserve army, to the extent and energy of accumulation, this law rivets the labourer to capital more firmly than the wedges of Vulcan did Prometheus to the rock. It establishes an accumulation of misery, corresponding with accumulation of capital. Accumulation of wealth at one pole is, therefore, at the same time accumulation of misery, agony of toil, slavery, ignorance, brutality, mental degradation, at the opposite pole.

Part 8
So-called Primitive Accumulation, and the Historical Tendency of Capitalist Accumulation

Chapters Twenty-Six to Thirty-Two

We have seen how money is changed into capital; how through capital surplus-value is made, and from surplus-value more capital. But the accumulation of capital presupposes surplus-value; surplus-value presupposes capitalistic production; capitalistic production presupposes the pre-existence of considerable masses of capital and of labour-power in the hands of producers of commodities. The whole movement, therefore, seems to turn in a vicious circle, out of which we can only escape by supposing a primitive accumulation preceding capitalistic accumulation; an accumulation not the result of the capitalist mode of production, but its starting point. This primitive accumulation plays in Political Economy about the same part as original sin in theology. Adam bit the apple, and thereupon sin fell on the human race.

The process, that clears the way for the capitalist system, can be none other than the process which takes away from the labourer the possession of his means of production; a process that transforms, on the one hand, the social means of subsistence and of production into capital, on the other, the immediate producers into wage-labourers. The so-called primitive accumulation, therefore, is nothing else than the historical process of divorcing the producer from the means of production. It appears as primitive, because it forms the pre-historic stage of capital and of the mode of production corresponding with it.

The economic structure of capitalistic society has grown out of the economic structure of feudal society. The dissolution of the latter set free the elements of the former. The immediate producer, the labourer, could only dispose of his own person after he had ceased to be attached to the soil and ceased to be the slave, serf, or bondman of another. To become a free seller of labour-power, who carries his commodity wherever he finds a market, he must further have escaped from the regime of the guilds, their rules for apprentices and journeymen, and the impediments of their labour regulations. Hence, the historical movement which changes the producers into wage-workers, appears, on the one hand, as their emancipation from serfdom and from the fetters of the guilds, and this side alone exists for our bourgeois historians. But, on the other hand, these new freedmen became sellers of themselves only after they had been robbed of all their own means of production, and of all the guarantees of existence afforded by the old feudal arrangements. And the history of this, their expropriation, is written in the annals of mankind in letters of blood and fire.

The industrial capitalists, these new potentates, had on their part not only to displace the guild masters of handicrafts, but also the feudal lords, the possessors of the sources of wealth. In this respect their conquest of social power appears as the fruit of a victorious struggle both against feudal lordship and its revolting prerogatives, and against the guilds and the fetters they laid on the free development of production and the free exploitation of man by man. The chevaliers d'industrie, however, only succeed in supplanting the chevaliers of the sword by making use of events of which they themselves were wholly innocent.

The starting-point of the development that gave rise to the wage-labourer as well as to the capitalist, was the servitude of the labourer. The advance consisted in a change of form of this servitude, in the transformation of feudal exploitation into capitalist exploitation. To understand its march, we need not go back very far. Although we come across the first beginnings of capitalist production as early as the 14th or 15th century, sporadically, in certain towns of the Mediterranean, the capitalistic era dates from the 16th century.

In the history of primitive accumulation, all revolutions are epoch-making that act as levers for the capitalist class in course of formation; but, above all, those moments when great masses of men are suddenly and forcibly torn from their means of subsistence, and hurled as free and "unattached" proletarians on the labour market.

The expropriation of the agricultural producer, of the peasant, from the soil, is the basis of the whole process. The history of this expropriation, in different countries, assumes different aspects, and runs through its various phases in different orders of succession, and at different periods. In England alone has it the classic form. The prelude of the revolution that laid the foundation of the capitalist mode of production was played in the last third of the 15th, and the first decade of the 16th century. A mass of free proletarians was hurled on the labour-market by the breaking-up of the bands of feudal retainers. The great feudal lords created an incomparably larger proletariat by the forcible driving of the peasantry from the land, to which the latter had the same feudal right as the lord himself, and by the usurpation of the common lands. The rapid rise of the Flemish wool manufactures, and the corresponding rise in the price of wool in England, gave the direct impulse to these evictions. Transformation of arable land into sheep-walks was, therefore, the cry.

The process of forcible expropriation of the people received in the 16th century a new and frightful impulse from the Reformation, and from the consequent colossal spoliation of the church property. The property of the church formed the religious bulwark of the traditional conditions of landed property. With its fall these were no longer tenable.

After the restoration of the Stuarts, the landed proprietors carried, by legal means, an act of usurpation, effected everywhere on the Continent without any legal formality. They abolished the feudal tenure of land, i.e., they got rid of all its obligations to the State, "indemnified" the State by taxes on the peasantry and the rest of the mass of the people, vindicated for themselves the rights of modern private property in estates to which they had only a feudal title, and, finally, passed those laws of settlement, which had the same effect on the English agricultural labourer, as the edict of the Tartar Boris Godunof on the Russian peasantry.

The "glorious Revolution" brought into power, along with William of Orange, the landlord and capitalist appropriators of surplus-value. They inaugurated the new era by practising on a colossal scale thefts of state lands, thefts that had been hitherto managed more modestly. These estates were given away, sold at a ridiculous figure, or even annexed to private estates by direct seizure. All this happened without the slightest observation of legal etiquette. The crown lands thus fraudulently appropriated form the basis of the today princely domains of the English oligarchy.

The last process of wholesale expropriation of the agricultural population from the soil is, finally, the so-called clearing of estates, i.e., the sweeping men off them. All the English methods hitherto considered culminated in "clearing." In Scotland areas as large as German principalities were dealt with. Part of the sheep-walks were turned into deer preserves.

The spoliation of the church's property, the fraudulent alienation of the State domains, the robbery of the common lands, the usurpation of feudal and clan property, and its transformation into modern private property under circumstances of reckless terrorism, were just so many idyllic methods of primitive accumulation. They conquered the field for capitalistic agriculture, made the soil part and parcel of capital, and created for the town industries the necessary supply of a "free" and out-lawed proletariat.

The proletariat created by the breaking up of the bands of feudal retainers and by the forcible expropriation of the people from the soil, this "free" proletariat could not possibly be absorbed by the nascent manufactures as fast as it was thrown upon the world. On the other hand, these men, suddenly dragged from their wonted mode of life, could not as suddenly adapt themselves to the discipline of their new condition. They were turned en masse into beggars, robbers, vagabonds, partly from inclination, in most cases from stress of circumstances. Hence at the end of the 15th and during the whole of the 16th century, throughout Western Europe a bloody legislation against vagabondage. Legislation treated them as "voluntary" criminals, and assumed that it depended on their own goodwill to go on working under the old conditions that no longer existed. Thus were the agricultural people, first forcibly expropriated from the soil, driven from their homes, turned into vagabonds, and then whipped, branded, tortured by laws grotesquely terrible, into the discipline necessary for the wage system.

The class of wage-labourers formed then and in the following century only a very small part of the population, well protected in its position by the independent peasant proprietary in the country and the guild organisation in the town. Variable capital preponderated greatly over constant. The demand for wage-labour grew, therefore, rapidly with every accumulation of capital, whilst the supply of wage-labour followed but slowly. A large part of the national product, changed later into a fund of capitalist accumulation, then still entered into the consumption fund of the labourer. Legislation on wage-labour (from the first, aimed at the exploitation of the labourer and, as it advanced, always equally hostile to him) is started in England by the Statute of Labourers, of Edward III, 1349. The ordinance of 1350 in France, issued in the name of King John, corresponds with it.

It was forbidden, under pain of imprisonment, to pay higher wages than those fixed by the statute, but the taking of higher wages was more severely punished than the giving them. A statute of 1360 increased the penalties. Coalition of the labourers is treated as a heinous crime from the 14th century to 1825. The barbarous laws against Trades' Unions fell in 1825 before the threatening bearing of the proletariat. Despite this, they fell only in part. Certain beautiful fragments of the old statute vanished only in 1859. During the very first storms of the revolution, the French bourgeoisie dared to take away from the workers the right of association but just acquired. By a decree of June 14, 1791, they declared all coalition of the workers as "an attempt against liberty and the declaration of the rights of man," punishable by a fine of 500 livres, together with deprivation of the rights of an active citizen for one year. This law which, by means of State compulsion, confined the struggle between capital and labour within limits comfortable for capital, has outlived revolutions and changes of dynasties. Even the Reign of Terror left it untouched.

As far as concerns the genesis of the farmer, we can, so to say, put our hand on it, because it is a slow process evolving through many centuries. In England the first form of the farmer is the bailiff, himself a serf. His position is similar to that of the old Roman villicus. Soon he becomes a half-farmer, advances one part of the agricultural stock, the landlord the other. The two divide the total product in proportions determined by contract. This form quickly disappears in England, to give place to the farmer proper, who makes his own capital breed by employing wage-labourers, and pays a part of the surplus product, in money or in kind, to the landlord as rent. To this, was added in the 16th century, a very important element. The continuous rise in the price of all agricultural produce swelled the money capital of the farmer without any action on his part, whilst the rent he paid (being calculated on the old value of money) diminished in reality. Thus they grew rich at the expense of both their labourers and their landlords.

The expropriation and eviction of a part of the agricultural population not only set free for industrial capital the labourers, their means of subsistence, and material for labour; it also created the home market.

Formerly, the peasant family produced the means of subsistence and the raw materials, which they themselves, for the most part, consumed. These raw materials and means of subsistence have now become commodities. The many scattered customers, whom stray artisans until now had found in the numerous small producers working on their own account, concentrate themselves now into one great market provided for by industrial capital. Thus, hand in hand with the expropriation of the self-supporting peasants, with their separation from the means of production, goes the destruction of rural domestic industry, the process of separation between manufacture and agriculture.

The genesis of the industrial capitalist did not proceed in such a way as that of the farmer. Doubtless many small guild-masters, and yet more independent small artisans, or even wage-labourers, transformed themselves into small capitalists, and (by extending exploitation of wage-labour and corresponding accumulation) into full blown capitalists. The snail's-pace of this method corresponded in no wise with the commercial requirements of the new world-market that the great discoveries of the end of the 15th century created. The Middle Age had handed down two distinct forms of capital, which mature in the most different economic social formations, usurer's capital and merchant's capital. The money capital was prevented from turning into industrial capital, in the country by the feudal constitution, in the towns by the guild organisation. These fetters vanished with the dissolution of feudal society, with the expropriation and partial eviction of the country population. The new manufacturers were established at seaports, or in inland points beyond the control of the old municipalities and their guilds.

The discovery of gold and silver in America, the extirpation, enslavement, and entombment in mines of the aboriginal population, the beginning of the conquest and looting of the East Indies, the turning of Africa into a warren for the commercial hunting of black-skins, signalised the rosy dawn of the era of capitalist production. These idyllic proceedings are the chief moments of primitive accumulation. On their heels treads the commercial war of the European nations, with the globe for a theatre. It begins with the revolt of the Netherlands from Spain, assumes giant dimensions in England's anti-jacobin war, and is still going on in the opium wars against China, &c. The different moments of primitive accumulation distribute themselves now, more or less in chronological order, particularly over Spain, Portugal, Holland, France, and England. In England at the end of the 17th century, they arrive at a systematical combination, embracing the colonies, the national debt, the modern mode of taxation, and the protectionist system.

These methods depend in part on brute force, e.g., the colonial system. But they all employ the power of the State, the concentrated and organised force of society, to hasten, hothouse fashion, the process of transformation of the feudal mode of production into the capitalist mode, and to shorten the transition. Force is the midwife of every old society pregnant with a new one. It is itself an economic power.

Of the Christian colonial system, W. Howitt, a man who makes a specialty of Christianity, says: "The barbarities and desperate outrages of the so-called Christian race, throughout every region of the world, and upon every people they have been able to subdue, are not to be paralleled by those of any other race, however fierce, however untaught, and however reckless of mercy and of shame, in any age of the earth." The history of the colonial administration of Holland — and Holland was the head capitalistic nation of the 17th century — "is one of the most extraordinary relations of treachery, bribery, massacre, and meanness."

The English East India Company, as is well known, obtained, besides the political rule in India, the exclusive monopoly of the tea-trade, as well as of the Chinese trade in general, and of the transport of goods to and from Europe. But the coasting trade of India and between the islands, as well as the internal trade of India, were the monopoly of the higher employés of the company. The monopolies of salt, opium, betel, and other commodities, were inexhaustible mines of wealth. The employés themselves fixed the price and plundered at will the unhappy Hindus. The Governor-General took part in this private traffic. Great fortunes sprang up like mushrooms in a day; primitive accumulation went on without the advance of a shilling. The treatment of the aborigines was, naturally, most frightful in plantation-colonies destined for export trade only, such as the West Indies, and in rich and well populated countries, such as Mexico and India, that were given over to plunder. But even in the colonies properly so-called, the Christian character of primitive accumulation did not belie itself. Those sober virtuosi of Protestantism, the Puritans of New England, in 1703, by decrees of their assembly set a premium of £40 on every Indian scalp and every captured red-skin: in 1720 a premium of £100 on every scalp; in 1744, after Massachusetts-Bay had proclaimed a certain tribe as rebels, the following prices: for a male scalp of 12 years and upwards £100 (new currency), for a male prisoner £105, for women and children prisoners £50, for scalps of women and children £50. Some decades later, the colonial system took its revenge on the descendants of the pious pilgrim fathers, who had grown seditious in the meantime. At English instigation and for English pay they were tomahawked by redskins. The British Parliament proclaimed blood-hounds and scalping as "means that God and Nature had given into its hand."

The colonial system ripened, like a hot-house, trade and navigation. The "societies Monopolia" of Luther were powerful levers for concentration of capital. The colonies secured a market for the budding manufactures, and, through the monopoly of the market, an increased accumulation. The treasures captured outside Europe by undisguised looting, enslavement, and murder, floated back to the mother-country and were there turned into capital. Holland, which first fully developed the colonial system, in 1648 stood already in the acme of its commercial greatness.

114

By 1648, the people of Holland were more overworked, poorer and more brutally oppressed than those of all the rest of Europe put together.

The system of public credit, i.e., of national debts, whose origin we discover in Genoa and Venice as early as the Middle Ages, took possession of Europe generally during the manufacturing period. The colonial system with its maritime trade and commercial wars served as a forcing-house for it. Thus it first took root in Holland. National debts, i.e., the alienation of the State — whether despotic, constitutional, or republican-marked with its stamp the capitalistic era. The only part of the so-called national wealth that actually enters into the collective possessions of modern peoples is — their national debt. The public debt becomes one of the most powerful levers of primitive accumulation. As with the stroke of an enchanter's wand, it endows barren money with the power of breeding and thus turns it into capital, without the necessity of its exposing itself to the troubles and risks inseparable from its employment in industry or even in usury.

With the national debt arose an international credit system, which often conceals one of the sources of primitive accumulation. Thus the villainies of the Venetian thieving system formed one of the secret bases of the capital-wealth of Holland to whom Venice in her decadence lent large sums of money. So also was it with Holland and England. By the beginning of the 18th century the Dutch manufactures were far outstripped. Holland had ceased to be the nation preponderant in commerce and industry. One of its main lines of business, therefore, from 1701-1776, is the lending out of enormous amounts of capital, especially to its great rival England. The same thing is going on today between England and the United States. The system of protection was an artificial means of manufacturing manufacturers, of expropriating independent labourers, of capitalising the national means of production and subsistence, of forcibly abbreviating the transition from the mediaeval to the modern mode of production. The European states tore one another to pieces about the patent of this invention, and, once entered into the service of the surplus-value makers, did not merely lay under contribution in the pursuit of this purpose their own people, indirectly through protective duties, directly through export premiums. The primitive industrial capital, here, came in part directly out of the state treasury.

Colonial system, public debts, heavy taxes, protection, commercial wars, &c., these children of the true manufacturing period, increase gigantically during the infancy of Modern Industry. The birth of the latter is heralded by a great slaughter of the innocents. A great deal of capital, which appears today in the United States without any certificate of birth, was yesterday, in England, the capitalised blood of children.

"From the different parish workhouses of London, Birmingham, and elsewhere, many, many thousands of these little, hapless creatures were sent down into the north, being from the age of 7 to the age of 13 or 14 years old. The custom was for the master to clothe his apprentices and to feed and lodge them in an "apprentice house" near the factory; overseers were appointed to see to the works, whose interest it was to work the children to the utmost, because their pay was in proportion to the quantity of work that they could exact. Cruelty was, of course, the consequence ... In many of the manufacturing districts, but particularly, I am afraid, in Lancashire, cruelties the most heart-rending were practised upon the unoffending and friendless creatures. They were harassed to the brink of death by excess of labour ... were flogged, fettered, and tortured in the most exquisite refinement of cruelty; ... they were in many cases starved to the bone while flogged to their work and ... even in some instances ... were driven to commit suicide ... The beautiful and romantic valleys of Derbyshire, Nottinghamshire, and Lancashire, secluded from the public eye, became the dismal solitudes of torture, and of many a murder. The profits of manufactures were enormous; but this only whetted the appetite that it should have satisfied, and therefore the manufacturers had recourse to an expedient that seemed to secure to them those profits without any possibility of limit; they began the practice of what is termed "night-working," that is, having tired one set of hands, by working them throughout the day, they had another set ready to go on working throughout the night; the day-set getting into the beds that the night-set had just quitted, and in their turn again, the night-set getting into the beds that the day-set quitted in the morning. It is a common tradition in Lancashire, that the beds never get cold."

What does the primitive accumulation of capital, i.e., its historical genesis, resolve itself into? In so far as it is not immediate transformation of slaves and serfs into wage-labourers, and therefore a mere change of form, it only means the expropriation of the immediate producers, i.e., the dissolution of private property based on the labour of its owner. This mode of production presupposes parcelling of the soil, and scattering of the other means of production. As it excludes the concentration of these means of production, so also it excludes co-operation, division of labour within each separate process of production, the control over, and the productive application of the forces of Nature by society, and the free development of the social productive powers. At a certain stage of development it brings forth the material agencies for its own dissolution. From that moment new forces and new passions spring up in the bosom of society; but the old social organisation fetters them and keeps them down. It must be annihilated; it is annihilated. Its annihilation, the transformation of the individualised and scattered means of production into socially concentrated ones, of the pigmy property of the many into the huge property of the few, the expropriation of the great mass of the people from the soil, from the means of subsistence, and from the means of labour, this fearful and painful expropriation of the mass of the people forms the prelude to the history of capital. It comprises a series of forcible methods, of which we have passed in review only those that have been epoch-making as methods of the primitive accumulation of capital. The expropriation of the immediate producers was accomplished with merciless Vandalism, and under the stimulus of passions the most infamous, the most sordid, the pettiest, the most meanly odious. Self-earned private property, that is based, so to say, on the fusing together of the isolated, independent labouring-individual with the conditions of his labour, is supplanted by capitalistic private property, which rests on exploitation of the nominally free labour; of others, i.e., on wages-labour.

As soon as this process of transformation has sufficiently decomposed the old society from top to bottom, as soon as the labourers are turned into proletarians their means of labour into capital, as soon as the capitalist mode of production stands on its own feet, then the further socialisation of labour and further transformation of the land and other means of production into socially exploited and, therefore, common means of production, as well as the further expropriation of private proprietors, takes a new form. That which is now to be expropriated is no longer the labourer working for himself, but the capitalist exploiting many labourers.

This expropriation is accomplished by the action of the immanent laws of capitalistic production itself, by the centralisation of capital. One capitalist always kills many. Hand in hand with this centralisation, or this expropriation of many capitalists by few, develop, on an ever extending scale, the co-operative form of the labour-process, the conscious technical application of science, the methodical cultivation of the soil, the transformation of the instruments of labour into instruments of labour only usable in common, the economising of all means of production by their use as the means of production of combined, socialised labour, the entanglement of all peoples in the net of the world-market, and this, the international character of the capitalistic regime. Along with the constantly diminishing number of the magnates of capital, who usurp and monopolise all advantages of this process of transformation, grows the mass of misery, oppression, slavery, degradation, exploitation; but with this too grows the revolt of the working class, a class always increasing in numbers, and disciplined, united, organised by the very mechanism of the process of capitalist production itself. The monopoly of capital becomes a fetter upon the mode of production, which has sprung up and flourished along with, and under it. Centralisation of the means of production and socialisation of labour at last reach a point where they become incompatible with their capitalist integument. This integument is burst asunder. The knell of capitalist private property sounds. The expropriators are expropriated.

The capitalist mode of appropriation, the result of the capitalist mode of production, produces capitalist private property. This is the first negation of individual private property, as founded on the labour of the proprietor. But capitalist production begets, with the inexorability of a law of Nature, its own negation. It is the negation of negation. This does not re-establish private property for the producer, but gives him individual property based on the acquisitions of the capitalist era: i.e., on co-operation and the possession in common of the land and of the means of production. In the former case, we had the expropriation of the mass of the people by a few usurpers; in the latter, we have the expropriation of a few usurpers by the mass of the people.

Other extracts from Capital

Aristotle and value (chapter 1)

Aristotle clearly enunciates that the money form of commodities is only the further development of the simple form of value – i.e., of the expression of the value of one commodity in some other commodity taken at random; for he says:

5 beds = 1 house

is not to be distinguished from

5 beds = so much money.

He further sees that the value relation which gives rise to this expression makes it necessary that the house should qualitatively be made the equal of the bed, and that, without such an equalisation, these two clearly different things could not be compared with each other as commensurable quantities. "Exchange," he says, "cannot take place without equality, and equality not without commensurability". Here, however, he comes to a stop, and gives up the further analysis of the form of value. "It is, however, in reality, impossible, that such unlike things can be commensurable" – i.e., qualitatively equal. Such an equalisation can only be something foreign to their real nature, consequently only "a makeshift for practical purposes."

Aristotle therefore, himself, tells us what barred the way to his further analysis; it was the absence of any concept of value. What is that equal something, that common substance, which admits of the value of the beds being expressed by a house? Such a thing, in truth, cannot exist, says Aristotle. And why not? Compared with the beds, the house does represent something equal to them, in so far as it represents what is really equal, both in the beds and the house. And that is — human labour.

There was, however, an important fact which prevented Aristotle from seeing that, to attribute value to commodities, is merely a mode of expressing all labour as equal human labour, and consequently as labour of equal quality. Greek society was founded upon slavery, and had, therefore, for its natural basis, the inequality of men and of their labour powers. The secret of the expression of value, namely, that all kinds of labour are equal and equivalent, because, and so far as they are human labour in general, cannot be deciphered, until the notion of human equality has already acquired the fixity of a popular prejudice. This, however, is possible only in a society in which the great mass of the produce of labour takes the form of commodities, in which, consequently, the dominant relation between man and man, is that of owners of commodities.

Bourgeois explanations of profit (chapter 7)

Our capitalist... exclaims: "Oh! but I advanced my money for the express purpose of making more money." The way to Hell is paved with good intentions, and he might just as easily have intended to make money, without producing at all...

He tries persuasion. "Consider my abstinence; I might have played ducks and drakes with the 15 shillings; but instead of that I consumed it productively, and made yarn with it." Very well, and by way of reward he is now in possession of good yarn instead of a bad conscience...

Besides, where nothing is, the king has lost his rights; whatever may be the merit of his abstinence, there is nothing wherewith specially to remunerate it, because the value of the product is merely the sum of the values of the commodities that were thrown into the process of production. Let him therefore console himself with the reflection that virtue is its own reward.

But no, he becomes importunate. He says: "The yarn is of no use to me: I produced it for sale." In that case let him sell it, or, still better, let him for the future produce only things for satisfying his personal wants...

He now gets obstinate. "Can the labourer," he asks, "merely with his arms and legs, produce commodities out of nothing? Did I not supply him with the materials, by means of which, and in which alone, his labour could be embodied? And as the greater part of society consists of such ne'er-do-wells, have I not rendered society incalculable service by my instruments of production, my cotton and my spindle, and not only society, but the labourer also, whom in addition I have provided with the necessaries of life? And am I to be allowed nothing in return for all this service?"

Well, but has not the labourer rendered him the equivalent service of changing his cotton and spindle into yarn? Moreover, there is here no question of service. A service is nothing more than the useful effect of a use-value, be it of a commodity, or be it of labour. But here we are dealing with exchange-value...

Our friend, up to this time so purse-proud, suddenly assumes the modest demeanour of his own workman, and exclaims: "Have I myself not worked? Have I not performed the labour of superintendence and of overlooking the spinner? And does not this labour, too, create value?" His overlooker and his manager try to hide their smiles.

The transformation of the working class (chapter 15)

Modern industry, by its very nature, necessitates variation of labour, fluency of function, universal mobility of the labourer; on the other hand, in its capitalistic form, it reproduces the old division of labour with its ossified particularisations. This absolute contradiction between the technical necessities of modern industry, and the social character inherent in its capitalistic form, dispels all fixity and security in the situation of the labourer... it constantly threatens, by taking away the instruments of labour, to snatch from his hands his means of subsistence, and, by suppressing his detail-function, to make him superfluous...

[Also] this antagonism vents its rage in the creation of that monstrosity, an industrial reserve army, kept in misery in order to be always at the disposal of capital; in the incessant human sacrifices from among the working-class, in the most reckless squandering of labour-power and in the devastation caused by a social anarchy which turns every economic progress into a social calamity.

This is the negative side. But if, on the one hand, variation of work at present imposes itself after the manner of an overpowering natural law, and with the blindly destructive action of a natural law that meets with resistance at all points, modern industry, on the other hand, through its catastrophes imposes the necessity of recognising, as a fundamental law of production, variation of work, consequently fitness of the labourer for varied work, consequently the greatest possible development of his varied aptitudes. It becomes a question of life and death for society to adapt the mode of production to the normal functioning of this law.

Modern Industry, indeed, compels society, under penalty of death, to replace the detail-worker of to-day, grappled by life-long repetition of one and the same trivial operation, and thus reduced to the mere fragment of a man, by the fully developed individual, fit for a variety of labours, ready to face any change of production, and to whom the different social functions he performs, are but so many modes of giving free scope to his own natural and acquired powers...

By maturing the material conditions, and the combination on a social scale of the processes of production, it matures the contradictions and antagonisms of the capitalist form of production, and thereby provides, along with the elements for the formation of a new society, the forces for exploding the old one.

Productive and unproductive labour (chapter 16)

[In capitalist society] the product ceases to be the direct product of the individual, and becomes a social product, produced in common by a collective labourer, i.e., by a combination of workmen, each of whom takes only a part, greater or less, in the manipulation of the subject of their labour. As the co-operative character of the labour-process becomes more and more marked, so, as a necessary consequence, does our notion of productive labour, and of its agent the productive labourer, become extended. In order to labour productively, it is no longer necessary for you to do manual work yourself; enough, if you are an organ of the collective labourer, and perform one of its subordinate functions...

On the other hand, however, our notion of productive labour becomes narrowed. Capitalist production is not merely the production of commodities, it is essentially the production of surplus-value. The labourer produces, not for himself, but for capital. It no longer suffices, therefore, that he should simply produce. He must produce surplus-value.

That labourer alone is productive, who produces surplus-value for the capitalist, and thus works for the self-expansion of capital... A schoolmaster is a productive labourer when, in addition to belabouring the heads of his scholars, he works like a horse to enrich the school proprietor. That the latter has laid out his capital in a teaching factory, instead of in a sausage factory, does not alter the relation.

Hence the notion of a productive labourer implies not merely a relation between work and useful effect, between labourer and product of labour, but also a specific, social relation of production, a relation that has sprung up historically and stamps the labourer as the direct means of creating surplus-value. To be a productive labourer is, therefore, not a piece of luck, but a misfortune.

An eleven-week study course on *Capital*

Week 1: Value and labour. Chapter 1 sections 1 and 2.

1. How would you define:
- commodity
- use-value
- value
- exchange-value
- abstract labour, or average social labour?

2. Why is average social labour the substance of value? What arguments against this theory do you know, and how would you answer them?

3. Can you think of any useful things which are products of human labour but not commodities?

4. What is 'the twofold nature of the labour embodied in commodities'? Why do you think Marx believed that this was 'the pivot on which a clear comprehension of political economy turns'?

Week 2: Commodity fetishism. Marx chapter 1 section 4.

1. Can you think of any examples of commodity fetishism in everyday speech?

2. How does commodity fetishism help to maintain a widespread acceptance of bourgeois ideas in the working class?

3. How does Marx's critical analysis of commodity fetishism contribute to communist politics?

4. Can you prove the labour theory of value?

Week 3: Money and prices. Chapter 1 section 3 and chapters 2 and 3

1. Marx says that Aristotle came close to solving the riddle of value, but was prevented by 'the historical limitation of the society in which he lived'. What do you think Marx meant?

2. List the forms of value that Marx analyses and give a short definition of each one.

3. How does money represent labour?

4. What's wrong with the usual economist's explanation of money as a mere convention to make exchange easier than it would be with pure barter?

Week 4: Capital, profit, and labour-power. Chapters 4, 5 and 6.

1. What is the purpose of the circuit C-M-C?

2. What is the purpose of the circuit M-C-M'?

3. Where do profits come from?

4. What's wrong with the idea that profits come from the capitalist's 'abstinence' in investing his wealth in production rather than consuming it straight off?

5. Are workers paid a fair wage? If so, how can we talk about exploitation?

6. Why say labour-power is bought and sold, rather than just labour?

7. What is wrong with the academic economists' definition of capital? 'Capital, in sum, is any previously produced input or asset of a business firm or any other producer' (Baumol).

Week 5: The working day. Chapters 7 to 11

1. During what period was the working day increased, and why?

2. During what period was the working day reduced, and why?

3. Marx's analysis depends on making a sharp distinction between human labour and the labour of other animals. If a farmer can produce more by e.g. using horses, Marx regards that as an increase in the pro-

ductivity of the farmer's labour, rather than a surplus gained by the farmer exploiting the horses' labour. Why?

4. What are constant and variable capital? And why does Marx call them that?

5. Why can't machines and raw materials add more than their own value to the product?

Week 6: Wages and profits. Read Marx's "Wages, Price, and Profit"

1. If workers win higher wages, what effect will that generally have on prices?

2. It's said that Marx predicted that capitalism would push workers into more and more absolute poverty and starvation. Did he really argue that?

3. What mechanism in capitalist society links wages to the value of labour-power?

4. What is the general guideline for Marxists active in trade unions?

Week 7: Cooperation and workshop division of labour. Chapters 12 to 14

1. After scattered handicraft production, Marx identifies two further stages of development of capitalist production prior to machine industry. How are each of these three stages defined?

2. Increased productivity of labour is, on the face of it, a good thing. Why is it not as simple as that for the workers?

3. Does capitalism promote or hinder routine large-scale cooperation in social production? Does that cooperation promote or hinder capitalism?

4. Why do the creative powers of the collective worker appear as the property of capital?

5. How can they come to appear as the workers' own property?

Week 8: Fully-developed capitalist industry. Chapter 15

1. What is the difference between a tool and a machine?

2. In his analysis of 'manufacture', Marx argues that it creates a workforce of narrowly specialised workers. Does modern machine industry do the same?

3. How does modern machine industry make 'abstract labour' a social reality rather than just one way of looking at labour?

4. If machinery enables less labour to produce more products, how is it that machine industry also enables and drives capitalists to lengthen the working day (as we saw in week 5) and intensify it?

5. In any social order, new technologies would devalue old skills, and cause difficulties for the workers specialising in those skills. So what is so special about capital's use of new technologies that under it 'the instrument of labour strikes down the labourer?'

6. In chapter 14 (in a passage not included in Rühle) Marx writes sarcastically against free-marketeer opponents of labour protection laws that: 'It is very characteristic that the enthusiastic apologists of the factory system have nothing more damning to urge against a general organisation of labour in society than that it would turn all society into one immense factory'. Does Marx himself want to turn all society into one immense factory?

7. Of modern industry Marx writes that: 'By maturing the material conditions, and the combination on a social scale of the processes of production, it matures the contradictions and antagonisms of the capitalist form of production, and thereby provides, along with the elements for the formation of a new society, the forces for exploding the old one'. Which elements? which forces?

Week 9: Wages; productive and unproductive labour; the reproduction of capitalist class society; unemployment; socialist revolution. Chapters 16 to 25 and 32.

In order to make more time in this course to study difficult and basic parts of *Capital*, a lot of material is telescoped into this week.

1. How does Marx define productive and unproductive labour? (See start of part 14, or chapter 16).

2. Which are unproductive?
a) A nurse in an NHS hospital; b) A nurse in a private hospital; c) A station supervisor on the London Underground; d) A bank clerk.

3. What is the value of labour? (See start of chapter 19).

4. In Capital (a passage not included in Rühle), Marx writes:
'Hence we may understand the decisive importance of the transformation of value and price of labour-power into the form of wages, or into the value and price of labour itself. This phenomenal form, which makes the actual relation invisible, and, indeed, shows the direct opposite of that relation, forms the basis of all the juridical notions of both labourer and capitalist, of all the mystifications of the capitalist mode of production, of all its illusions as to liberty, of all the apologetic shifts of the vulgar economists'. (See chapter 19).

5. Which is better for the worker, time-wages or piece-wages? (See chapters 20 and 21).

6. What does the process of capitalist production, repeated week after week, year after year, yield for the workers? And for the capitalists? (See chapter 23).

7. Why does capitalism have a constant tendency towards mass unemployment? (See part 23, chapter 25).

8. How does capitalism pave the way for socialist revolution? (See chapter 32).

Week 10: How capitalism got going. Capital chapters 26 to 32

1. Compared to the feudal serf, the wage worker is more free in a straightforward sense. How? And also more free in a sarcastic or ironic sense. How?

2. Marx argues that the rise of the capitalist farmer and of the industrial capitalist involve different stages and factors. Which different stages and factors?

3. Why is it only half-true to present the rise of bourgeois society as a battle for liberty against feudal and guild restrictions?

4. When did capitalism first appear? In what ways was it then not fully-fledged?

5. Were there capitalists and capital before capitalism?

Week 11. Marxism vs bourgeois alternatives and criticisms

Below are three propositions argued by an early advocate of modern orthodox economics, Stanley Jevons, in contrast to Marx's views. For each of the three, summarise the alternative Marxist view, and examine the arguments on both sides.

1. Value is decided by marginal utility (the utility of the last extra bit of a commodity consumed), not by labour-time. In fact, this is the same as saying that it is decided by supply and demand.

Although Jevons does not use the word 'marginal' in the excerpt given, that is what he means, and he was in fact one of the pioneers of the concept. In reply to the objection that diamonds are much more valuable than apples or loaves or shirts, though apples or loaves or shirts are much more useful, Jevons would point out that diamonds are bought only when people, having few or none of them, decide that one more diamond is worth more to them than extra of the apples and loaves and shirts of which they already have lots. People can make that comparison, and, in fact, having limited budgets, constantly do make that comparison.

The more apples (or diamonds) are produced, the more people get to the point where they really would prefer lots of other things to more apples (or diamonds), and the lower the average 'marginal utility' of apples falls. When it falls as low as the cost of production, then supply equals demand, and marginal utility equals cost of production equals price.

2. The production of wealth needs land, labour and capital, not just labour.

3. The owner of each factor of production - land, labour, or capital - must be paid for his factor's contribution to production. How much they are paid is determined by supply and demand, not by any process of exploitation.

Jevons: archive.workersliberty.org/wlmags/capital/ex10a.htm

Notes and extra reading:
archive.workersliberty.org/wlmags/capital/course.htm

Further reading

More on the 11-part course — bit.ly/capital-awl

Further notes and resources on all three volumes of *Capital*, including critical notes on David Harvey's lectures on volume 1 — bit.ly/3-vols

David Harvey on volume 1 — davidharvey.org/reading-capital/

David Harvey on volume 2 — davidharvey.org/2012/01/marxs-capital-vol-2-class-01/

Karl Kautsky's summary and explication of *Capital* volume 1 — www.marxists.org/archive/kautsky/1903/economic/index.htm

Rosa Luxemburg's summary of *Capital* volumes 2 and 3 — www.marxists.org/archive/mehring/1918/marx/ch12.htm#s3
Karl Korsch's introduction to *Capital* volume 1 — www.marxists.org/archive/korsch/19xx/introduction-capital.htm

Nicole Pepperell on the opening chapters of *Capital* volume 1 — bit.ly/nicole-pep

Marx's Capital, by Ben Fine and Alfredo Saad-Filho, 5th edition — bit.ly/fine-sf

Harry Cleaver's guide to *Capital* volume 1 — webspace.utexas.edu/hcleaver/www/357k/357ksg.html